Put Your Hand in My Hand...

The Spiritual and Musical Connections of Catherine and Gene MacLellan

Harvey Sawler

NIMBUS
PUBLISHING
NIMBUS.CA

Nimbus Publishing Limited
3660 Strawberry Hill Street,
Halifax, NS, B3K 5A9
(902) 455-4286 nimbus.ca

Printed and bound in Canada

NB1291

Interior Design: Peggy & Co
Front Cover Design: Kevin Vail, Prevail Creative

Library and Archives Canada Cataloguing in Publication

Sawler, Harvey, 1954-, author
Put your hand in my hand : the spiritual and musical connections
of Catherine and Gene MacLellan / Harvey Sawler.

Put your hand in my hand.
ISBN 978-1-77108-581-6 (softcover).—ISBN 978-1-77108-582-3
(HTML).

1. MacLellan, Gene. 2. MacLellan, Gene—Family. 3. MacLellan, Catherine.
4. Composers—Canada—Biography. 5. Singers—Canada—
Biography. I. Title.

ML410.M167S28 2018   782.42164092   C2017-907983-2
                                        C2017-907984

Nimbus Publishing acknowledges the financial support for its publishing activities from the Government of Canada, the Canada Council for the Arts, and from the Province of Nova Scotia. We are pleased to work in partnership with the Province of Nova Scotia to develop and promote our creative industries for the benefit of all Nova Scotians.

For Judith, Catherine, and Isabel

Give me something to write about
and I'll write you a song.

—Previously unpublished, from Gene MacLellan's personal journals

Give me something to write about
and I'll write you a song

CONTENTS

A 1971 playbill for Gene MacLellan soon after he became famous for his international hit songs "Snowbird" and "Put Your Hand In the Hand."

INTRODUCTION

I never set out to create a trilogy of books focusing on the lives of Atlantic Canadian performance and recording artists. It's just the way opportunity presented itself, first with a series of coincidences resulting in the writing of *On the Road with Dutch Mason* (with co-author and my former band mate, Dave Bedford) in 2005 and then the 2016 sojourn and release of *One Man Grand Band*, the authorized biography of the late Newfoundland and Labrador singer-songwriter Ron Hynes.

The Catherine and Gene MacLellan book idea actually preceded the others. I first approached Catherine about this project nearly eleven years ago. I was a long-time admirer and was full of curiosity about Catherine's father, Gene. And when I discovered Catherine for the first time, I found her to be an irresistible dichotomy: a young woman whose offstage persona seemed the opposite of a singer-songwriter, musician, and performer. I'd dealt with those people for years professionally as a performing-arts publicist, but Catherine was not like any of the others—there was not a *showy* bone in her body. She was soft, quiet, reserved, full of humility, and, it seemed at the time, vulnerable. I would come to learn that she was very much, in these and many other respects, her father.

Catherine was courteous enough to see me and discuss the idea of a book, which would explore the musical and spiritual connections between her and her father. It was just a hypothesis at the time, one which would prove itself out. Although she never really flat out said "no," I think we both sensed that the timing was just not right. She had just had a child, she was eking out her space within the Island music scene, the relationship with her partner had grown unstable, and I had other book projects on the go.

Scroll ahead to 2012 and a Gene MacLellan tribute concert that was staged and produced for CBC Radio and TV at the Zion Presbyterian Church in downtown Charlottetown. The production featured the talents of several PEI singers and songwriters, including Lennie Gallant, Meaghan Blanchard, and Dennis Ellsworth, as well as Newfoundland's "Man of a Thousand Songs," Ron Hynes, and, of course, Catherine. My fascination with Catherine and Gene was reborn as I watched that CBC production live and then later that summer on television.

Four years later, I again approached Catherine. Much had changed in her life. Her daughter Isabel had grown into a preteen, as mature and independent for her age as anyone could ever imagine to be. Catherine was in a very positive place—her music career was growing, she was involved in a good personal relationship, and she had more or less come to terms with her relationship with Gene. Concurrently, the producers of the Cavendish Beach Music Festival and the owners and management of the PEI Brewing Company—who are one and the same—were asking me and others, no doubt, to contribute ideas for a summer-long musical showcase which might feature Island artists. I pitched them the idea of Catherine creating a musical tribute to her father. The book and such a production, I hoped at the time, might coincide.

Happily, the PEI Brewing Company people and Catherine loved the idea. As I set about to interview for and write the book, Catherine set about to negotiate with the company and shape and write the proposed stage production. The publishing business being what it often is, one took longer than the other—after a hard winter's work with her collaborators, Catherine's tribute, *If It's Alright With You*, premiered on July 3, 2017, at the PEI Brewing Company and ran for thirty-one shows, selling out most nights to enthusiastic audiences. It is no surprise that the show has been rebooked for the summer of 2018.

Put Your Hand In My Hand was still being written at the time I got to see Catherine perform and to witness how audiences embraced her remarkably honest renditions of Gene's songs and her stories about life with him and without him. Most poignantly, she revealed how she gradually came to terms with Gene's place in her life, her music, and their music, after his January 1995 suicide.

In the years between my first pitch to Catherine and her eventual agreement to collaborate on the book, she had gone on to record and release a substantial body of work of her own, and she had become a road warrior, performing across Canada, in the States, and in Europe. She independently released two albums: 2004's *Dark Dream Midnight* and 2006's *Church Bell Blues* before signing to True North Records, which re-released *Church Bell Blues* in 2007. She followed up with *Water in the Ground* in 2009. *Dark Dream Midnight* was included as a bonus disc with physical copies of that album. She toured North America and the United Kingdom throughout 2009 to support the album and was engaged for performances on CBC Radio's *Canada Live* and *The Vinyl Cafe*. Her album *Silhouette* was released by True North Records in July 2011, followed by the release of *The Raven's Sun* in August 2014. She has also participated in two collaborative Canadian Songbook tours: in 2008 with Murray McLauchlan, Stephen Fearing, and Paul Quarrington, and in 2009 with McLauchlan, Barney Bentall, and Nathan Rogers. In November 2009, she recorded a new song, "Singing Sands," for CBC Radio 2's Great Canadian Song Quest. And of course in June of 2017, she released the tribute album to Gene, *If It's Alright With You*, which would mirror the PEI Brewing Company stage production.

She'd also strung together a fine list of awards: winner of both Female Solo Recording of the Year and Folk Recording of the Year, and a nomination for SOCAN Songwriter of the Year at the 2010 East Coast Music Awards; winner of Folk Recording of the Year and nominations for Album of the Year and Solo Recording of the Year at the 2012 East Coast Music Awards; winner of English Songwriter of the Year at the 2012 Canadian Folk Music Awards; winner of Solo Artist of the Year at the 2009 Canadian Folk Music Awards; Number One Roots Artist on iTunes Canada; PEI winner of CBC Radio 2—Canadian Song Quest; Penguin Eggs—New Artist Discovery of the year in 2008; 2015 Juno Award for Roots & Traditional Album of the Year—Solo for *The Raven's Sun*.

Catherine had more than made her indelible mark on the Canadian music scene.

It's my belief that in spite of the personal and musical independence Catherine has discovered for herself, she is never really without Gene, both on a personal level and on a musical level. He is omnipresent. During one-on-one interviews and throughout her live Charlottetown tribute production, she told story after story that drove this belief home.

But there's one small story that is left for Catherine's mother, Judith, to tell. It's about the remarkable day that Gene took his then thirteen-year-old daughter on the ferry from Wood Islands, Prince Edward Island, to Caribou, Nova Scotia. Famed singer Anne Murray was hosting a musical get-together of the old CBC *Singalong Jubilee* crowd at her Nova Scotia summer cottage. Although Catherine was several years away from performing at any level, Gene apparently told Murray he had a daughter who could sing. She was really just singing around the house at the time, like any teenager would. But Judith believes there was a latent musical connection there between father and daughter even then.

"He just knew it, and I think that's where their connection came from."

Like her father, Catherine has a quiet charisma and a pure voice. (Photo by Rob Waymen)

PART 1 - LIFE

And I know sometimes you feel like you can't go on

But you can make it

You just take up your cross and follow Jesus

Take up your cross every day

Don't be ashamed to say that you know him

Count the cost, take up your cross, follow him

—Untitled, unpublished lyrics from Gene MacLellan's personal journals

CHAPTER 1

HEAVEN MUST BE UNIMAGINABLE

Catherine Ruth MacLellan was born on April 23, 1980, to Gene and Judith MacLellan.

She learned to read by reciting passages of the Bible during sleepovers at her grandmother's place. Gene's mother's family were fairly severe Kirk of Scotland Protestants and, ironically, their religion allowed no music in church. Catherine learned to read through phonics as well, of course, but her first practical reading was time spent with her grandmother through the Good Book. She didn't have to wait for heaven to receive her reward for having done so.

"I got an award for having read one hundred pages of the Bible," she recalls.

Although she can no longer recall or recite those passages, Catherine remembers that the Psalms were pretty.

"And I liked Revelations because it was exciting. Scary, actually!"

The Bible was a large part of Gene's life, and the MacLellan kids were well exposed to church, Sunday school, and learning the scriptures.

A family photo of the three MacLellan children, Rachel, Philip, and Catherine, with their parents, Judith and Gene. (Courtesy of MacLellan family)

Today, however, Catherine is not the least bit religious.

"I spent my childhood caught up in that," she explains. "That's good enough for me....I grew up deeply entrenched in it. Now it seems like a day at the dentist.

"I don't believe in a God who punishes us for our behaviour. I don't believe in a God who has favourites, who says one person is good and one person is bad. I don't believe in heaven or hell. I don't know what I believe, but I know what I don't believe, including the notion that there is a supreme being."

Her mother, Judith, and Gene, however, were very religious and they were religious together, you might say. Because of the depth of their shared devotion and outlook, one would think Catherine might have followed a like path. According to Judith, however, the death of her father threw Catherine for such a life-altering loop that it caused her to question any possibility there might be a God.

Rather, one of Catherine's favourite theories, based on a book she recently read, is the idea of emergent phenomenon, a good example of which she says are ants.

"They have these huge colonies of tens of thousands of ants, but one ant on its own really is no good at anything and couldn't do anything for himself, really. But they can take care of building these massive, really well-organized colonies. Someone's getting the food. Someone's taking care of the children—like, they are really amazing. So it is like this collective consciousness, I guess."

She doesn't see emergent phenomenon as a religion. It's more of a philosophy or an idea of how society has been formed.

"It's like my origin story, maybe," she says. "We start off with intentions maybe just to get food, shelter, or fire, or whatever, but the more we collect-ively have these intentions, good or bad, the more we shape the entire world."

Religion to her father, on the other hand, was an immense, if not intense, aspect of his life. Gene was immersed in his Lord. Catherine thinks Gene's go-to version of the Bible was the King James.

"He would go and lock himself in his little den or office, or even once I remember he had this big room that he set up as an office, and went in there and fasted and read the Bible for what felt like forever, but it may have just been like a couple of weeks."

Gene could fast up to seven to ten days at a time, drinking just sugar water to keep his systems functioning. Catherine has the sense that he was cleansing himself on two fronts, physically and spiritually. Sometimes he would fast without secluding himself away, being around the family home while avoiding sustenance other than his consumption of the Bible. Catherine, her siblings, and Judith could see him getting skinnier by the hour. For her part, Catherine has made attempts at fasting, but loves food too much for it not to be a part of her lifestyle.

⁕ ⁕ ⁕

Gene did not take all of his religiousness with him when he took his own life on January 19, 1995, at the age of fifty-six. He left behind songs of spirituality, songs praising his Lord, and a random collection of journals, dog-eared Hilroy scribblers, and pocket-sized hardcover notebooks—copious notes which reveal

I SING MY SONG FOR JESUS
AND I NEVER ASK FOR PAY
FOR IT'S PAY ENOUGH
TO SERVE SOMEBODY WHO LOVES YOU
THOUGH THE SUN BE SHINING BRIGHT
OR THE SKIES BE FILLED WITH GREY
I'LL BE SINGING MY SONG FOR JESUS EVERYDAY

I'LL SING MY SONG FOR JESUS
THOUGH THE ONES WHO HEAR BE FEW
I DON'T NEED MEN'S APPLAUSE FOR INSPIRATION
AND I DON'T NEED MY NAME UP IN LIGHTS
FOR I'VE SEEN WHAT THAT CAN DO
YES IT LONELY UP THERE AT THE TOP
WHEN "THE LAUGHINS" ALL THROUGH

much of how he viewed the world and his God within it. Catherine has the box full of those writings at her home on the Dixon Road, a 5.5-kilometre stretch of road in the rural, earthy, central Prince Edward Island community of Breadalbane. She opened the door to some of her dad's most personal thoughts by sharing them for this book.

Catherine says that her dad wasn't very organized, so a lot of his thoughts and writings were scattered. There were other journals and writings Gene had set ablaze for some reason or another, probably during one of his most depressed or vulnerable times. It's a shame these were lost, for who knows what else they might have revealed about him and his beliefs, his world, his loves, and his losses. Who knows what songs may have been lost when he burned those memories.

"He was very creative," says Catherine. "He had bursts of creativity," which is what the journals exemplify, as well as his feelings about God and religion. Religion was a cornerstone of Gene's life and of his writings.

"I think he used religion as part of his therapy," she says.

On Friday, October 26, 1990, he wrote in the voice of his alter ego, Willard, the protagonist in an uncompleted novel MacLellan had worked at off and on for several years.

"Heaven must be unimaginable," Willard wonders, reflecting, of course, Gene's own wonderings over what life must be like after death. The line captures for us an image of Gene spending time thinking about heaven, visualizing heaven, dreaming of heaven.

Catherine thinks Willard "was a barely veiled version of my father. He was my dad."

So who was Willard and just who was Gene MacLellan?

According to Catherine and to Gene's journals, Willard was a shy, quiet guy who had a lot of health problems as a child.

Gene wrote about Willard, "You are my creation and my responsibility," describing his subject as being fifty-two years of age but looking at least sixty-two. "Small and thin, he had lived hard until he was almost forty." Gene describes Willard as a writer working on a Halifax-based television show, which he portrays as an intense, stress-filled experience. "He had lived with an almost perpetual fear in his gut for the most part of his miserable life."

Willard's persona and his similarities to Gene became clear to Catherine when Gene would read pieces of the unfinished work to her or sparingly talk now and then about the book project. The fact that he shared aspects of Willard and his novel with Catherine suggests that he felt close enough to share more with her than many fathers and daughters ever do.

Gene also wrote and spoke to God frequently in his own voice.

"Dear Lord," he wrote in one of those scribblers, "I know you've commanded us not to be anxious about anything. But sometimes I get this feeling that I might have moved ahead of your plan for my life."

No one knows, of course, what Gene meant by such passages. Given the way his life came to a close, one can do well to only imagine.

Gene always wrote about Willard as being in some kind of pain: "Pain and suffering is inevitable, but misery is optional."

Catherine, more than anyone, probably because she is a writer in her own right, pays the most attention to these writings and is the one most left to consider what they might have meant and what value they hold. She doesn't obsess over or over-analyze them, but it's hard to ignore them. They are intriguing and thought-provoking, whether you're Gene's daughter, or a casual observer, or an author.

As his Lord is a mystery, Gene is a mystery. And because he is gone and we can't ask him to elaborate, Gene's images of heaven are unimaginable.

Jesus said he loved me so
I believe that, you know
Sure I believe in the ghost, I believe in the sun
I believe that we all were holy once
But now our sins are catching up
From our father's drinking cup
To the oldest of wines that we pour from the flask
The things that we should but we never do ask

— "SOMETHING GOLD" BY CATHERINE MACLELLAN

CHAPTER 2

The Noise

To members of a certain generation, most of whom have grey hair, Gene MacLellan is a Canadian cultural icon who wrote songs with penetrating lyrics and inescapable melodies, a distant-yet-familiar figure who gave them many musical memories and remains close on a personal level. To newer generations, he is, naturally, far less interesting, that is until Catherine sits at her piano or picks up her guitar and, in her particular style, contemporizes her father's works.

This is Gene's gift to Catherine and subsequently her gift to new audiences who deserve to become familiarized with that Canadian icon and to hear the eloquent lines from MacLellan songs like "The Pages of Time" in which he wishes he could turn back time to the love "that was mine." Through this song and so many other of his compositions, we can feel Gene's pain. It is through Catherine now that we turn back the pages of her father's time and peer into his soul and musicality.

A rare photo of a young Gene, centre, making music with friends. (Courtesy of Ray Dart)

There is no generational divide when it comes to lyrics such as those found in "The Pages of Time." Given the right performer, the right voice, and the right orchestrations, any divide can be erased. Catherine and her audiences have explored this theory and proven it to be so.

There is also no typifying divide when it comes to the business Catherine and Gene both found themselves caught up in—the music business. The fundamentals of that business have not changed much over the decades of modern music: it is a raucous, callous subculture of society and, really, one big noisy place—not always a place for nice people. That two people like Gene and

Catherine entered into and resided within that culture is certainly contrary to most music industry norms.

American singer Brenda Lee once said: "The music business can be very cold. And it doesn't honour its elders." According to legendary Canadian singer-songwriter Joni Mitchell, an idol of Catherine's, "I heard someone from the music business saying they are no longer looking for talent; they want people with a certain look and a willingness to co-operate." Even in the seventeenth century, Italian composer Claudio Monteverdi said: "Music is spiritual. The music business is not."

But American journalist and author Hunter S. Thompson, most renowned for his best-known work, *Fear and Loathing in Las Vegas: A Savage Journey to the Heart of the American Dream*, summed it all up when he wrote that "the music business is a cruel and shallow money trench, a long plastic hallway where thieves and pimps run free, and good men die like dogs. There's also a negative side."

So how did Gene wind up in the music business?

He began his career as a young singer and guitarist in 1956 with the popular Toronto rock band Little Caesar and the Consuls. Three years later, the five-piece group split in two, with three members, Gene, Robbie Robertson (to become internationally famous with The Band), and Peter Deremigis, forming The Suedes. Bruce Morshead and Norm Sherrat eventually put a new band of Consuls together.

Gene's road to the top was a winding one. He moved to Pownal, Prince Edward Island, in 1964 and worked as an orderly in a psychiatric hospital at the same time he was teaching himself to write songs. His big break came when he made an uncharacteristically brash bid to get the attention of Don Messer, going to Messer's Nova Scotia home with bass player Blair Doucette to demo a quick song. The overture to Messer worked: the next thing Gene and Doucette knew they were being featured on *Don Messer's Jubilee*, the once-popular CBC Television music, song-and-dance-filled variety show produced in Halifax but seen across Canada. Next were his appearances on what was originally the summer replacement for the Messer show, the Halifax production *Singalong Jubilee*,

ENTERTAINMENT

Gene MacLellan leaves his farm to face the fans

By BRUCE KIRKLAND
Star staff writer

A young woman walked up to a shaggy-haired, slightly built man in the Royal York Hotel this week and asked the inevitable question with the fan's look of hushed expectancy: "Are you really Gene Mac-Lellan?"

It wasn't exactly a moving moment in MacLellan's life but still, it was important. It was recognition, the warning sign that the public has made MacLellan a star and brought him to Toronto for a concert at Massey Hall tomorrow night.

"I don't want to ask you for your autograph or anything," the woman was saying, "but I'd like to tell you I think you're an excellent singer."

HIT TUNE

It wouldn't have happened if the 34-year-old composer of Anne Murray's biggest hit, Snowbird, (she get's first choice of any song he writes), and the rock group Ocean's only hit. Put Your

ing one night stands with Little Caesar and the Consuls.

He has since worked as a dishwasher in Toronto, where he grew up after leaving his birthplace, Val D'Or, Quebec, at the age of two, and as a hospital attendant in Charlottetown, where he moved eight years ago because Toronto was too busy, too much.

The tour now is a change, though. "The more you write songs the more introverted you become. To get out of it you have to stop writing," MacLellan said. "But when my privacy runs out, that's the time to quit."

Like a hundred other struggling artists, he tells you:

"I'm not out to make a big bundle." Yet coming from MacLellan, it sounds genuine. "I wouldn't know what to do with it even if I did make a lot. I've never had much money."

It's been two years since he recorded his album and four since he wrote Snowbird (the second he ever

COMPOSER of Snowbird, Anne Murray's greatest hit, Gene MacLellan got a surprise visit this week from the singer who gets first choice of any song he writes. Mac-Lellan is in Toronto for concert at Massey Hall row night. It's been two years since he reco album and four years since he wrote Sn

A *Toronto Star* newspaper story explores Gene's reluctant stardom, four years after "Snowbird" made him famous. Shown with Gene is Anne Murray, the artist most identified with the international hit.

where he met soon-to-be internationally acclaimed recording artist Anne Murray, the favourite daughter of Springhill, Nova Scotia.

Success came fast and almost out of nowhere after he penned two songs that immortalized him in the annals of Canadian music and, for a time, made him a good bit of money—"Snowbird" (as recorded by Murray) and "Put Your Hand in the Hand" (as recorded by the Toronto rock band Ocean). He could sit and watch Murray sing their hit on the sensational CBS network variety show *The Glen Campbell Goodtime Hour* or tune into any top-forty station and hear Ocean's rendition of "Put Your Hand in the Hand."

The two songs brought him swiftly to national attention. It is said that "Snowbird" was only his second composition and was written in about twenty-five minutes, and that he had Murray in mind. It went on to become one of North America's most played songs of 1970. That was the year Gene was awarded the Juno Award as composer of the year, one in a string of recognitions he would receive during his lifetime and posthumously.

"Put Your Hand in the Hand" was a gospel pop song first recorded by Murray for her third studio album, *Honey, Wheat and Laughter*. Released by Ocean as the title track to their debut album, their single peaked at No. 2 on the US *Billboard* Hot 100 and went on to become the twenty-second-best seller of 1971. The song was more recently used in the 2013 film *Prisoners*.

"Put Your Hand in the Hand" was recorded by more than one hundred artists, including Elvis Presley, Frankie Laine, Andy Williams, Perry Como, Chet Atkins, Chris Connor, Joan Baez, Sammy Davis Jr., Alden David, Cactus Country Band, Loretta Lynn, the Oak Ridge Boys, Randy Stonehill, and the unlikely combination of Bing Crosby and Count Basie for their 1971 album, *Bing 'n Basie*. South African singer Ray Dylan recorded a cover on his album *Goeie Ou Country-Op Aanvraag*. In a 1991 episode of the sitcom *Family Matters* titled "Choir Trouble," the cast sang the song in their church as part of their gospel fest. "Put Your Hand in the Hand" had became a solid standard of the gospel repertoire internationally.

Throughout the early 1970s, Gene was immersed in the music scene, following the Murray and Ocean exposure by recording his own LP, *Gene MacLellan*, which included the more modest but equally resilient hits "The Call" and "Thorn in My Shoe."

There was a string of concert appearances at places like the Canadian National Exhibition and Toronto's Massey Hall; an eventual second LP, *If It's Alright with You*, released in 1977; and a third LP, *Gene & Marty*, a collection of gospel songs with close friend and collaborator Marty Reno, which was issued in 1979.

But even as Gene's compositions grew nearly as familiar to popular and easy-listening audiences as the Canadian national anthem, he was gradually distancing himself from the clamour. A change overcame him, and he chose to leave music for five years. Unassuming and spiritual by nature, Gene is noted by all who knew him for having eschewed the spotlight for a more quiet lifestyle. He was uneasy with success and periodically disappeared from public view. He was no Elvis Presley. At the very time that his compositions were being recorded by stars all over the world and during which his fame was peaking, Gene was looking for solace, comfort, and an escape.

In the 1980s and 1990s, Gene kept a low public profile. He gave performances in churches, penitentiaries, and retirement homes. He appeared on gospel broadcasts and PEI cable TV programs and he reached out to prison inmates. Gene's formal appearances were rare—he did attend Anne Murray's induction into the Juno Hall of Fame in 1993, and he was at a SOCAN ceremony that declared "Snowbird," "The Call," and "Put Your Hand in the Hand" Canadian classics.

"Gene and I were fairly new in our relationship, and so he did not speak much about his feelings regarding the business," says his widow, Judith. "I think he felt pressured by the record company to tour and then to complete his contract with them. He just did not enjoy all the fuss, especially when touring. He once said he would be happiest if he could be in a recording studio twenty-four hours a day. As he was a private person, the quiet or the lack of the spotlight very much appealed to him."

The PEI Songwriters Association made him an honorary life member; even today he would stand as the association's elder statesman. But for the most part, Gene was seeking a way out of the limelight and felt that only his God could give him that peacefulness.

Open up the door, drop the keys to the floor
It's been a long day
Turn the sheets down on the bed, I've got nothing left to give
It's been a long day

—"Winter Spring" by Catherine MacLellan

i've got a wife and three kids

Food enough to fill a fridge

A Bible on the table

About a mile from skyway bridge

As the crow flies more or less

I make my living from the past

Don't know how long things can last

—"I've Got A Wife and Three Kids," unpublished lyrics
from Gene MacLellan's personal journals

CHAPTER 3

Thorns in Their Shoes

The MacLellan family moved around a lot, their many moves being linked to Gene's transient life. As Catherine says, he was "a rambler."

So although all three kids were born in different places, they all ended up with their last childhood stop being on Prince Edward Island. Catherine and brother Philip remain there, as does their mother, Judith. Catherine's sister, Rachel (Evans), was born in 1977 and lives today in Kingston, Ontario, with her husband, Jeff, and two kids. Rachel plays piano and a bit of guitar, and sings.

"She has kept the religious tradition alive for our family," says Catherine. "She plays in her church in kind of a modern church band."

Philip, a sound- and recording-studio guy, was born in 1974 and lives in Summerside, with his wife and five kids.

Philip is not only a sound technician. He also writes songs.

"He writes really beautiful songs," says Catherine. "Really sensitive."

I've got a wife and three kids
Plenty in the Fridge

I'VE GOT A WIFE AND THREE KIDS

~~I've~~

I've got a wife and three kids

I've got a wife and three kids.
Food enough to fill a fridge
A Bible on the table
About a mile from Skyway bridge
as the crow flies, more or less
I make my living from the past
Don't know how long things can
last
I make my living from the past,
and I'm really not addicted
to the fast lane.

Out of Burlington
I make my living from the
past
And I'm really not addicted
to the fast ways.

But they're not in her repertoire. For one thing, she's probably only heard them once or twice and she has enough material between her own and her father's to keep any set list fresh and engaging.

"They're his songs. They are his voice. They don't express the way I see the world."

Plus Catherine believes she will keep writing forever.

❄   ❄   ❄

"This is where my mom went to high school," Catherine says about PEI. "My grandparents ended up staying here, so that's kind of part of the reason we are from the Island."

Catherine and her family moved around so much that she estimates living in about fifteen or sixteen different houses in her life, as though she had been a military brat like her mother. It was not unfamiliar practice for either her father or mother. Gene's childhood had been unusually transient, Judith's more predictably so because of her father being in the air force.

Gene's parents met in the 1930s in Boston, but neither of them was from there. After they met, they moved quickly back to Canada and started looking for work.

"And you know the Depression and all of that economy—they were kind of struggling to make a living so they just went wherever the work was," says Catherine. "My grandfather was from the Gaspé Peninsula in a place called Richmond near Black Cape, and then my grandmother, Catherine Chandler, was from the Pownal area of PEI.

"My grandfather started working in the mines in Val-d'Or, Quebec, which is why my dad was born there. He also sold insurance, sold real estate, sold all kinds of stuff over the years. Eventually, the family wound up in Toronto, which is where Gene really grew up."

"He was a city boy," Catherine explains, appreciating that most people, and especially Islanders who like to lay claim to Gene, are surprised by or sometimes tend to be in denial of that fact.

"So we just never stayed put. We were never satisfied with where we were. We just always thought there was somewhere else we should be."

With all the family's moving about, Catherine attended a lot of different schools in places like Burlington and Oakville in Ontario: Park Avenue Academy for kindergarten, Oakville Christian School for grades one through four, Tecumseh Public School in Burlington for grades five and six. Gene and Judith split for a period and when they reunited in October of 1990, the family moved back home to PEI. At certain points in his life, it seems there was always something drawing Gene back to PEI, the place of his mother's origins.

That's when Catherine was delivered to what is now Athena Consolidated School in Summerside for grades six through nine before heading on to Three Oaks Senior High School to complete her school years. Ironically, more than twenty years earlier, Athena is where Anne Murray was working as a physical education teacher before her exposure to Gene, her break onto CBC's *Singalong Jubilee*, her rise to US network television, and the worldwide fame that rapidly unfolded for her.

Catherine always seemed to know she wasn't cut out for the academic scene.

"I was the kind of kid who didn't really have to work too hard to get a B. I didn't really study too much. I was pretty good at everything, especially art and music, but I just showed up and did my projects last minute and always got a decent mark. I don't know if it was harder for my dad."

As has been the case for most of her life, there was no master plan, whether it was her disinterest in going to university, ambling from job to job when she was younger, or anticipating the next phase of her music career.

After a life-altering escape to Australia (following Gene's death) and a short period at Dalhousie University in Halifax, Catherine returned to Summerside and began working at the then-Jubilee Theatre, now the Harbourfront Theatre.

"A woman who was stage manager went on maternity leave, and my brother, Philip, was working there full-time, so I just kind of got this part-time gig working there. Then the lighting guy there was my brother's best friend. He was going to Toronto to work in theatre, and I just hopped in this bus with him. We were friends, also, and we got this crappy apartment in Toronto, and

A young Gene with his sister, Joan (now Boyington), and his parents, Philip and Catherine (nee Chandler). (Courtesy of MacLellan family)

he actually worked in theatre for real, and I got a few gigs. You know, lights, teardowns. It's pretty funny. I ended up working at Toronto's Second City Theatre selling tickets.

"It was awesome," says Catherine. "I loved it."

She stayed for the better part of a year before boomeranging back to Summerside and a folk café job at Spinnaker Landing on the city's waterfront. Her friend Dave Gould had opened the place. She started getting up doing a song or two and began dating her co-worker James Phillips. Next thing they knew they were forming a four-piece band called The New Drifts, with Phillips on guitar and mandolin, Stéphane Bouchard on bass, and Dave Gould on drums and percussion. The New Drifts did a few covers and as Catherine puts it, "more eclectic stuff." Forming the band marked the end of any form of normal working life, as it led eventually to the derring-do of her solo career.

"It was just kind of a broadening of relationships too."

She says that meeting people in the music scene becomes your sense of normalcy.

"It just becomes life," she says. "And then suddenly, you don't have other jobs."

It's been thirteen years since Catherine's held down a "normal" job, working at a newly opened Global Pet Foods store in Charlottetown, only then because she desperately needed work. Like selling tickets at Second City, she was more or less a cashier and, again, she loved the experience.

"I loved it because I got to go and play music all the time and kind of filled that part of my life, and just to throw bags of dog food around. I got to learn a bit about dog food, animal food, pet food, and pets. I love animals," which is a trait she may have picked up from her dad, who had a penchant for photographing dogs, including his mother's dogs and their own family pet, Skippy, a dog he had since before Catherine can remember. There were always dogs showing up in Gene's photos.

"He loved animals," says Catherine. "He loved dogs for sure; I know that."

The pet-food store job was fun for Catherine because she was working with animals and serving people who loved animals—and she got a paycheque for doing so. Those jobs were mostly about having money, of course, versus the deeper love of songwriting and performing. At the end of the day, you have to have sustenance, something her dad never should have had to fret over after he wrote "Snowbird" and "Put Your Hand in the Hand." He was basically all set. But worry he did.

"He was very bad with money, so he worried a lot about it," says Catherine. "It would all be gone by the time the tax bill came around or whatever."

The "Snowbird" and "Put Your Hand in the Hand" royalties were for a while powerful.

"They aren't anymore," she says, "but at that time, yeah. Plus he was still getting gigs and he was still playing music back then here and there."

One key difference between Gene and Catherine is that she is, it seems, firmly and permanently ensconced in Breadalbane, perhaps breaking the MacLellan family cycle of a transient lifestyle. The grass is quite green enough on her side of the Dixon Road, thank you, especially since she and her musical and personal partner, Chris Gauthier, have built an on-site recording studio where they can continue to create new music. The studio is a labour of love, mostly attributable to Chris, who Catherine says is "good at everything" including carpentry and other building skills.

Almost the only noise to be heard at Catherine's place, which Gene would have deeply appreciated, is the sound of music emanating from her and Chris's studio.

We never stayed in one place, just couldn't stick around
It's in our blood it seems, No we can't tie ourselves down
Go from home to home and town to town

— "ALL THOSE YEARS" BY CATHERINE MACLELLAN

Don't need a high profile
Just wanna be invisible
Just wanna leave in style
A body indivisible

—Untitled, unpublished lyrics from Gene MacLellan's personal journals

CHAPTER 4

THE QUIET

It is no coincidence that there is a softness and quietness about Gene's lyrics, now reflected stylistically in so much of Catherine's persona and her work.

He was a very quiet man. A man who had a deep appreciation for silence. He understood how to be in a silent place. In spite of the sometimes-raucous industry he was engaged in, this quietness, this softness, this appreciation for silence, endured for Gene and has also emerged as an important aspect of Catherine's day-to-day existence. She remembers her father's warmth of spirit, as though she'd been exposed to it just yesterday. Next to music, you could call it her other inheritance, derived from the countless positive memories she retains of their lives together.

Catherine says her father was a simple man who would have preferred gardening, fishing, and cooking to living in the complex, frequently damaging music industry. Although he was known publicly for his music, those who truly knew him say Gene's humility, love, gentleness, caring, kindness, and generosity were his real personal calling cards.

Even the way Gene dressed was simple and humble.

"He was very old-fashioned in that way," says Catherine, and one might add the word "conservative." "He almost never left the house without a suit jacket on, like a tweed suit jacket with those elbow patches. It was just his style."

Catherine's style is simple too. She is reliably found in jeans and a T-shirt or jeans and a button-up shirt. A big transition for her in the summer of 2016 was the idea of wearing shorts.

Gene MacLellan would give you the warmth of the shirt off his back. Literally. Catherine relates several stories about her father's generosity, including the time during one particularly chilling winter that he gave the insulation from his garage to a friend who needed insulation for his house. That friend was the late PEI musician Kim Vincent.

"Kim was a fabulous violin player," according to musical friend Lennie Gallant, whose point of view about music is one of the most credible in Atlantic Canada. Gallant is an Island-born singer-songwriter and musician whose style crosses into the folk, Celtic, rock, and country music genres, and whose social outlook is captured in the words from his Ottawa Order of Canada induction as an artist who can "articulate the feelings of many caught up in desperate situations beyond their control, and at the same time celebrate the beauty of lifestyle and landscape with their strong poetry and stirring narratives."

"It's a shame he never had records out of his own," says Gallant about Vincent. "He is as good as anybody on the planet. Kim lived out in Granville there, not very far from the [Gene's] famous workshop out there. Kim and Gene were good buddies. Gene recognized great talent in him.

"Kim was working putting together a workshop and Gene went over to visit him," says Gallant. "Winter was coming on, I guess. I don't know the exact details, but the winter was coming on and it was cold. Gene said, 'Kim, you've got to get some insulation in here.' Kim was living hand to fist to mouth all the time. He was barely getting by.

"Gene had insulation that was meant for his studio. He took it over and gave it to Kim because he felt Kim needed it more. And so he took his own insulation from his studio and gave to Kim."

Catherine has attempted to find the calm, the balance in life, that eluded her talented father. (Photo by Rob Waymen)

It was Kim who told Gallant the story first-hand.

"Kim and I sang in that shack," says Gallant.

PEI craftsperson and musician Malcolm Stanley, a fixture of the arts scene on the Island for four decades, experienced Gene's warmth and generosity a year after he and his wife, Christine, moved there in 1977.

Shortly after arriving on the Island, Stanley was hitchhiking home from New Brunswick when Gene picked him up. It apparently mattered not to Gene, conservative in his appearance, that Stanley had long hair and a beard. This was when the PEI ferry was still in service between Cape Tormentine, New Brunswick, and Borden-Carleton, Prince Edward Island. So the two had time for lunch together on the boat.

Stanley recalls Gene talking about the person you appear to be in public—referring to his fame and popularity—not amounting to a "hill of beans" when it comes to who you really are when you're at home living your life with your family. Stanley told this story to Catherine years later and it rang familiar with her—Gene apparently used the expression "hill of beans" quite regularly.

When the ferry was docking, Gene offered to drive Stanley all the way to his home at the time in Oyster Bed Bridge, not terribly inconvenient, but not exactly next door to where Gene was living either. Gene said he needed to check in at the house with Judith and to see the kids, Philip and Rachel (Catherine was not yet born). During their stop, a big man with a beard showed up. Stanley thinks that this person had to be Jack MacAndrew, Gene's manager at the time and a close friend. For the half an hour that Gene and the big, bearded man talked, Stanley whiled away the time by strumming Gene's Gibson guitar, which Catherine has in her possession today.

Stanley never forgot Gene's kindness, generosity, and approachability.

✶   ✶   ✶

Gene was quiet and often silent, but Catherine says he was also the funniest person she's ever met. He took his work seriously but never himself.

JUNE 20/87
(SOMETIME BETWEEN 11:30-12:PM

'THE DOOR'

A MILLION SNOWFLAKES FLAKES FALLIN'
NONE OF THEM THE SAME
EACH ONE WITH IT'S OWN DESIGN
BUILT IN A SILVER FRAME FOR ALL TO SEE
AND I DON'T NEED TO BE A SCIENTIST BLOWS
TO FEEL YOUR BREATH AS IT GENTLY FALLS
                                    UPON ME

"When he was home and not on the road, he would just be home with us—things like driving us to school and taking us out for junk food," she says. "He was just a sweet and gentle soul, and I got to spend a lot of time with him in the last couple of years before he died, and that was a really special time."

Gene also took his time with everything he did. Living and acting against the societal grain, he never rushed.

"And he always had time for us three kids," says Catherine, reflecting on special "Gene" and family stories that linger.

"He always had time for me."

Gene taught Catherine the association between time and listening. He was, as she puts it, a great listener.

✳ ✳ ✳

Again characteristic of this pursuit of quietness and the need to pace one's life, Catherine is trying to use her time wisely. She wants to be more organized than her father was.

"I'm working on it," she confesses. "It's my lifetime goal to be creative, but to keep my head on straight."

Many would argue that being creative is like having a licence to be disorganized. Catherine agrees with that observation, but argues that it shouldn't be.

"Some of the most successful people in my peer group are also the most organized. Rose Cousins is the biggest example. She is almost too good in business because it sometimes stops her creativity. I'd like to find a balance. Jenn Grant is more in the middle. Like she's definitely more flighty than Rose, but definitively does a good job keeping things rolling."

There isn't as much free time for Catherine as it might appear to onlookers, who see her gigs as being sporadic, leaving most of her days free.

"Firstly, for me, one of the challenges is trying to become more organized and trying to get more work done so I can continue having more of a career in music. Ask retired people, the ones who aren't bored. Like there is no more time after you retire; your time is taken up in other tasks. It does allow me in

Gene MacLellan

jeani read *music*

hard to reach

Gene MacLellan hides inside 34 years of difficult living that he doesn't like to talk about, beneath a painful need to be reserved about his thoughts and faithful to his secrets. Talking to him is something of a breathless minuet. The atmosphere is rarefied. This is a very private man.

The austere, hastily-assembled mask of his face can be both boyish and weary, but is always watchful. Suspicions of betrayal. Something steps carefully through the air between the mask and the questions with a warning: don't ask if you don't care about the answers.

Anne Murray's recording of his Snowbird sold more than two million copies and was done by nearly 100 other art-

ists. Put Your Hand in The Hand, by Ocean, sold more than four million and was done by 70 artists. But there are many other handfuls of candor and perception and beauty in his collection besides. About the only clear access to Gene MacLellan is through his music itself. And he doesn't even like to talk about that. You have to listen to the songs.

For the last year, MacLellan has sequestered himself on a farm 25 miles outside of Charlottetown, on Prince Edward Island. He feels his roots are there, in spite of being born in Quebec and being raised in Toronto. He lives with his wife, 12 cats and two dogs.

But one somehow feels that the only

person MacLellan lives with, really, is himself.

"I've been in and out of the business for the last 12 years. I started with a group called Little Caesar and the Consuls, before it was called Little Caesar and the Consuls. I was second string guitar player. You know who the first string guitar player was? Robbie Robertson, of The Band. That's why I was second string. I was really bad and he was really good." MacLellan sketches out his memories quickly and wryly.

"I'd be singing other people' songs, but I was never good enough to be hired for good jobs. When you get that laid on you, then you don't consider yourself a singer. When I started writing I found out what I was — and to me that's writing."

After three years with the Consuls, MacLellan moved from Toronto to Rhode Island, where he attended a Bible school and travelled throughout the New England states with evangelist Bud King — an experience to which he attributes much of the influence for songs like Put Your Hand in The Hand.

"That was just one experience in my life. I don't know why I went — I just felt it was a need then I'm not religious, but I'm spiritually inclined."

Work in a mental institution also deeply influenced MacLellan's vision. "At first it was just a job that was there, but when I got in I was glad because I know a lot of really intelligent people who were in there. They had serious problems, but I learned a lot from them. I made some very good friends. They were so honest it wasn't funny. It was very scary sometimes. They would tell me things about myself that I knew were pretty accurate, and so I know they were thinking people. They helped me and maybe I helped them, I don't know.

"It was hard emotionally to see that much pain and suffering, but I stuck it out for the best part of three years.

I think it affected my writing. I think if I write about sorrow, for instance, I'm writing about somebody else's as well as my own. Probably more somebody else's."

Acutely nervous on stage — "It's terrible being an introvert," he will mutter into the microphone, and it is all too

his music, you may be rewarded with an anecdote. Like the time he went to L.A. "I was down there once, on a promotional thing. And that was a sham. I got talked into going down there on a vacation. It wasn't what they had said. They had a whole bunch of things lined up, like radio stations and that.

If they had told me before, it would have been all right. I would just have said no. But it caused trouble for both of us."

MacLellan, you see, just borrowed a friend's motorcycle and eluded the promotion men in the hills. He doesn't take well to being treated like a product.

"I led what some people would probably call a sheltered life up until pretty late in life. I'm going through some changes now just like you are, probably. If I come out on the other side I'll be able to tell you about them. If they help me, maybe I can pass them on.

"I'm not a chicken writer. I write exactly what I feel. I can't write about anything I'm unsure of. Then I feel uncomfortable. I have to write exactly what I see in front of me.

I don't understand what Snowbird means. Most of the songs I've written I can understand when I look back on them. But I never understood Snowbird. I wrote it in such a short time that I should have understood it, but I don't."

Snowbird took all of 20 or 25 minutes to write. It doesn't usually take much longer. Not, says Gene, if it's the right

This newspaper story, written when Gene was thirty-four, exposes his vulnerability. Speaking of his time working in a psychiatric hospital, he admits that it was "hard emotionally to see that much pain and suffering."

the long run to have more time for creativity, and I think that was my dad. He was always doing something. He never was idle. He had time on his hands to do nothing with."

He would be reading or working on various household projects, although she says he wasn't very handy.

Catherine has pursued things other than her music to occupy her life. She has developed the ability to complete a project within a certain amount of time. As an example, she took up sewing several years ago, making quilts, a few dresses, skirts, and shirts.

"They were okay. I need practice. I need years of practice."

And quilts are no small feat. They take a long time to make, which she compares to making an album.

Being self-employed in the music business is one of the most precarious pursuits a person can attempt, especially if you're trying to go it alone. Catherine has been through the mill of having people help her. Her first manager was Lloyd Doyle of Charlottetown, who was key during her early evolution when things were at the very beginning. Following Doyle, she went without a manager for a period, eventually working with Grady Poe, who lived in the Evangeline region in western PEI.

"Grady kind of came on as an intermittent guy to help me get through that stage. I've been working with a guy called Shawn Russell from Toronto. But I'm kind of feeling at this point right now that self-management makes more sense. Having a manager in Toronto doesn't make a lot of sense for me. I need meetings to be face-to-face and that only happens once or twice a year. It's like phone calls and emails," which doesn't help her feeling organized, grounded, or in control.

She knows what she's in for with the self-management routine, having attempted it between her time with Doyle and Poe. For the last record she put out, she was self-managed.

"I think if you have an agent to help you book shows—and I have several throughout the different regions I play in—that helps. And that's part of my goal for becoming more organized. Because I don't make a ton of money, giving 15 or 20 percent of that away to somebody doesn't make a lot of sense when it's never very clear if they are making a difference or not."

The booking agents take on many artists at a time and book them throughout a particular region. So, she has one in Canada, another in the Netherlands, a person who helps her out in Germany, and another one in Ireland. She had a guy in England who fell ill and is no longer working.

Gene's long-time manager was the late prolific public-relations man and media personality, the aforementioned Jack MacAndrew. A journalist whose claim to fame was covering the 1956 Springhill coal-mine disaster for CBC

Radio, MacAndrew was also once the national producer of English variety entertainment for the CBC, including productions such as *The Tommy Hunter Show* and CBC *Superspecials*. MacAndrew knew his way around PR, entertainment, and media and was an important figure in Gene's career, as well as being a close friend back on the Island. In fact, MacAndrew was Catherine's daughter Isabel's great uncle because his wife, Barbara, is sister to the late Reverend Robert Tuck. Reverend Tuck's son, Al, is Isabel's father.

Catherine's mother, Judith, reflects that up until the late '70s, the first part of Gene's career, somebody else was always leading and in control of Gene's direction in the music business. Although one side of MacAndrew's personality mirrored Gene's in that they both loved rural life on PEI, MacAndrew was also ambitious and gregarious enough to always seek the limelight, if not controversy. He was widely known as an outspoken newspaper columnist and CBC Radio commentator and political critic. There is a possible dichotomy here. While Gene wanted to vanish from the public landscape, MacAndrew (and others) may have been constantly pulling him back onto it. MacAndrew publicly acknowledged his love for Gene, but once a promoter always a promoter. Knowing MacAndrew myself on a personal and professional level for many years, I believe it might have driven him nuts for Gene not to capitalize on his talent.

"I don't think he expected anything even close to what he got," says Judith. "I didn't know him at the time, but knowing Gene, I'd say, no. He was just happy if someone would just play his songs other than him."

Judith believes that from Catherine's earliest beginnings in the business, especially compared with Gene, she has had more to say about where she wants to go.

"We don't talk about her business very much. We just talk about family," says Judith, but she is observant enough to know that Catherine has chosen certain managers and agents for certain reasons, and if they weren't doing their respective jobs, then she would not hesitate to cut ties.

✳   ✳   ✳

Gene was a shy person who, in spite of his ability to perform and the widely acknowledged effect of his subtle charisma, wasn't comfortable around crowds. He loved people, but preferred one-on-ones or house parties.

"You wouldn't find him seated and having coffee at Tim Hortons," as the late Newfoundland and Labrador singer-songwriter Ron Hynes put it. "He'd use the drive-thru."

Judith says that Gene would have been more happy and at ease at home, and playing his songs to smaller groups.

"To play in front of, you know, hundreds of people was not his style," says Judith. "He really loved playing with people at house parties."

Judith was the complete counter to Gene's reserved nature. She is the self-professed talker in the family.

"I'm the one who will spout anything to anybody!" she says.

Judith also did not share the quiet, peaceful nature of both Gene and Catherine. For example, when she and Gene fought, Judith admits, she was loud. This seems to her to be an extension of the tendency among Judith and Catherine's brothers and sisters to "fight at the drop of a hat over nothing," as she puts it, something that Catherine has never joined in on.

✳   ✳   ✳

Catherine takes after her father. Quiet and shy since she can remember, where she lives is indicative of her demeanour. The Dixon Road is in all respects peaceful and still, a place that offers a very simple existence that Catherine shares with Isabel and Gauthier. The three have been together now for eight years.

Isabel is Isabel Louella MacLellan, a very with-it young lady with an independent disposition, named in part after Catherine's mother's mother, Louella. Her aforementioned father, Al Tuck, is a singer-songwriter from Summerside, who for part of his career was based in Halifax.

Judith reflects on Isabel, one of her eight grandchildren.

"She's been a little adult since she's been walking and talking. Whatever she decides to do, she is going to be the best at."

There seems to be a consensus that Isabel is more assertive and direct and less prone to quietness than Catherine or Gene.

Today when Catherine is travelling for gigs and other commitments, Isabel usually goes with her father, or Judith helps out, or the girl stays on the Dixon Road with Gauthier.

"It's changing all the time. It's never the same," says Catherine. But the situation is very manageable now. It doesn't hurt that Isabel has that independent streak and seems mature for her age.

Gauthier is from Mayfield, PEI, near the north shore harbour community of North Rustico. He and Catherine met through music.

"I had another guitar player for years, and he was unable to play with me, so I was looking for someone to fill in for this guy, and the first time I asked Chris, he said no. He was playing in a band called Paper Souls and then he moved to Toronto or, actually, he moved to Scotland and then he moved to Toronto. And then he moved home. He was just playing for various people like Mitch Schurman and Chas Gay, and playing with people around, so I saw him and asked him again. So, from then he became the only constant, except when I moved to Halifax I started playing with some other guys, but even at the end of that, Chris started playing with me again.

"It's definitely meant to be. We always had other partners. I never thought of him that way until suddenly we were both single."

For a girl born in Canada's Golden Horseshoe, Catherine is extraordinarily rural, if not back-to-the-land, in her outlook and lifestyle. Rural is deep in Catherine's bones. The MacLellan family lived on Walker Avenue in Summerside, which before it was developed was behind a farm field, so it felt like the city's outskirts. But very rural Millvale is where Gene really wanted to be and where he began building a recording studio, which evolved into a combined studio and home. Judith on the other hand was a city girl, born a Pickard in Montreal to an air force photographer and his wife.

Catherine, who lives with her daughter and her partner, Chris Gauthier, in rural PEI, has pursued quietness while controlling the pace of her music career. (Photo by Jule Malet-Veale)

While Gene was out doing music, Judith was busy at home raising the kids. She was at home until Catherine was five or six years old, finally taking a path toward several part-time secretarial and administrative-assistant types of jobs in the order of eighteen to twenty hours per week, which she still continues to do.

Rural PEI is where Catherine, Philip, and Rachel (mostly she and Rachel) lived for a period during one of Gene and Judith's domestic splits. He'd already had the studio in a log cabin in Granville, not far from Millvale. This is where her grandparents were living, so Catherine would be there for weeks on end when she and her siblings came home from Ontario during the summer.

Catherine says there is a unique sense of closeness amongst herself, her mother, and her brother and sister. The family relocations and other events, especially the tragedy of Gene's death, are things they went through together.

"We all did go our separate ways, but we've kind of stayed close. Maybe it is just the thread of family."

Before settling on the Dixon Road, Catherine had bounced around between the Island and other places after high school.

"When Isabel was born, I left here and went to Halifax. I spent two years there and I just had this desire to come home. I didn't even know it until one day I was out by Millvale where my dad's place was. There is this heritage road that I love taking. It is just so beautiful. It was September, and I stopped to pick an apple and I left my car on the side of that little road and I walked into the field beside it and just kind of felt like this is where I have to be. I felt the Island was calling me home.

"Not because of its safety, but because of how much it has to offer. I guess after growing up in a transient household with transient parents, I just really wanted to put down some roots and to be nourished by the land here and the community here. So, I knew that I wanted to be either here or a satellite neighbourhood of Millvale."

Breadalbane has an eclectic assortment of lefties, whom writer Sandra Phinney once referred to as "actors and artists, carpenters and clowns, foresters and filmmakers, weavers and writers, print makers and playwrights, singers and sheep producers," and who find themselves living out the old Island saying, "We're so far behind, we're ahead."

Catherine jokes that the Dixon Road is like the suburbs of Breadalbane. Here, atop a small hill at the end of a climbing, angled lane is Catherine's simple two-storey house.

To describe Catherine's house as "simple" is an understatement. The more apropos word is "sparse." While the kitchen is well enough equipped, the remainder of the downstairs is a showcase of minimalist living: a small set of table and chairs, a small couch, a corner chair, and a worn wooden floor. One gets Catherine right away when at her place—she couldn't care less about materialistic things. She is into her daughter, her partner, her friends and family, and her music. Period.

She came across the house thanks to her late neighbor Hal Mills, who founded The Dunk (named for the Dunk River), Breadalbane's locally renowned performance and music venue and also the site of Mills's home. He was very much responsible for Catherine's current lifestyle.

"He [Hal] called me up," she recalls. "I was in Ottawa for a show, and he said, 'You've gotta check out this house.' I came back to visit the Island, and Hal came with me, and we looked at this house, and I didn't really like it at first."

It had vinyl siding, so it wasn't exactly the earthy motif she romanticized over with the Granville log cabin.

"It just wasn't what I imagined my life to be."

But the setting and rural atmosphere compensated for the vinyl siding. Plus she and Gauthier had more than enough space to erect the adjacent studio, found through a small thicket of trees just above the house.

The twelve years she's been there is the longest she's lived anywhere in her entire life. She is absolutely a bona fide citizen of the area, a "Dixon Roader" as they call themselves locally.

"It's quiet," says Catherine. "I love it here. I have really great neighbours. There is usually a potluck or campfire to go to, or people to learn gardening from or any other skill that you might need."

And of course, they all share a love for music. The very first musical event at The Dunk was in 2005 with Funk the Dunk: A Celebration of Music, Food and Friends. This has become an annual event, held every May on the Sunday of the Victoria Day long weekend. Including other events such as Summer Solstice, DunkStock, Winter Solstice, the Annual Pie-off & Musical Extravaganza, and House Concerts, The Dunk has become a gathering place for the Dixon Road community of friends—a place to enjoy music and to support musicians. The first House Concert (thought to be a one-off) was for Catherine MacLellan in May 2008. Before noon the next day The Dunk received an email from singer-songwriter Brooke Miller saying, "I hear you do house concerts," and the rest, as they say, is history. During the 2009 calendar year, more than forty musical events were hosted at The Dunk.

Some affectionately refer to Catherine as "the darling of The Dunk."

When Mills died in 2015, his life was celebrated with a long day and evening of performances, stories, laughter, and tears and, of course, that proverbial PEI rural potluck dinner.

Gene would no doubt love to be where Catherine is today, keeping life quiet and simple. He would have loved to be playing music with his daughter and people like Hal Mills and the earlier-mentioned hitchhiker Malcolm Stanley, a fixture in the area for decades, and recording songs in the studio on the hill overlooking Catherine's home. Gene would have been a true Dixon Roader.

> Staying way up in the mountains.
> Where it's so hard just to breathe
> Everything looks like a miracle.
> So hard to believe.
>
> —"Eastern Girl" by Catherine MacLellan

Lately I've been runnin' on faith
What else can a poor boy do
But my world will be right
When love comes over you
Lately I've been talking in my sleep
Can't imagine what I'd have to say
Except my world, be right
When love comes back my way

—"Runnin' on Faith," unpublished lyrics from
Gene MacLellan's personal journals

CHAPTER 5

BROTHERHOOD
SISTERHOOD

Marty Reno was Gene's brother, not by bloodline, but in spirit. Today at seventy-seven, Reno has countless memories of his old friend—the times their families actually lived together, their relentless touring and performances, their writing songs and recording together. When he's not golfing—to which he is terribly addicted—or sailing with friends like singer-songwriter Tom Gallant, Reno lives today in Niantic, near New London, Connecticut, about halfway between Boston and New York on the Long Island Sound. While doing this interview, Reno, Gallant, and two other buddies were waiting for a window of good weather to sail Gallant's forty-seven-foot schooner from Lunenburg, Nova Scotia, to Bermuda and ultimately on to the Caribbean.

Born in Montreal but raised on PEI, Reno was a fixture on the Canadian music scene for decades, acquiring his first guitar at just nine years of age, and growing up travelling and performing across Canada, in the US, in Europe, and in the Caribbean. Like Gene, he formed a band as a teenager, just two

RUNNIN' ON FAITH

1 Lately I've been runnin' on faith
What else can a poor boy do
But my world will be right
When love comes over you

2 Lately I've been talkin' in my sleep
Can't imagine what I'd have to say
Except my world be right
When love comes back my way

CHORUS: I've always been one to take each and every day
Seems like ~~I'd find~~ by now
I'd find a love who cares
Cares just for me

3 And we'd go runnin' on faith
All of our dreams would come true
And our world would be right
As love comes over me and you

Instru. break...

CHORUS

3

years later than his protégé, in 1958. Reno concentrated on covering such country-music artists as Marty Robbins, Johnny Cash, and Hank Williams, including an extended touring run of the popular musical-theatre production, *Hank Williams: The Show He Never Gave*. He would inevitably focus on gospel and sacred music, primarily with Gene.

The two met at some point shortly after Gene's appearances on *Singalong Jubilee* had run their course on CBC Television. Reno can picture their first encounter, although he can't quite remember the year.

Gene was back on the Island. Although they weren't acquaintances, they lived only a few kilometres from another — Gene living in the south shore Island hamlet of Pownal and Reno in the increasingly suburbanized Southport (now Stratford), across the Hillsborough River from Charlottetown. Gene knew Reno to see him because Reno had been playing around Charlottetown and parts of the Island for years. Reno, with his wife and his cousin, ran into him in a grocery store.

"So he came to my cousin's house," recalls Reno. "We sat around the table and got our guitars out. He would play a song for me, and I'd play a song for him."

Gene was enthralled. Reno was enthralled.

They kept swapping songs back and forth that they'd just written.

"We became instant friends. From that point on, if I wasn't at his house, he was at mine. We would just play and play."

Gene told Reno one day that he had three commitments to fulfil, one of which was an appearance on CBC's perennially popular variety production *The Tommy Hunter Show*. Gene didn't want to get a big band together because he didn't envision staying on the road. He was tired, according to Reno, so Reno as accompanist was a more manageable, less stressful way for Gene to fulfil his commitments.

There was a magic moment during which Gene and Reno truly realized that they were destined to become friends and musical collaborators. Driving to Toronto, Gene reached into his pocket and pulled out a little Gideons New Testament version of the Bible.

"He held it out to me and I reached into my pocket and pulled one out as well. That was it!"

The two Bibles were identical, giving rise to the mutual acknowledgement that they should be collaborating by making a mutual decision to ease away from singing and performing commercial material in favour of gospel songs.

"We sort of became reconnected through our spiritual beliefs about the same time," says Reno. "He had always been well-connected spiritually, and he had sort of re-devoted his life at one point."

This spiritual connectivity reflected not only where they wanted to go musically, but also in terms of their lifestyles. Both wanted to escape the rat race. But before making a fully dedicated shift to gospel and sacred music, there were those remaining obligations Gene had to get out of the way.

Reno became Gene's guitar accompanist and there's no doubt, according to East Coast music personality Eric MacEwen, that "he was brilliant" in that role.

"He also became a best bud," says MacEwen. "Gene was quiet and gentle and Marty understood this. He also understood that Gene was a giant of a songwriter. I once complimented Marty on his guitar-playing techniques as I had only rarely seen and heard such dexterity and seamless skill in a guitarist."

But Reno felt he didn't hold a candle to Gene, and MacEwen couldn't much argue, talking about the old 1920s and '30s guitar chords and riffs Gene employed in the melodies to his songs, "for they are genius."

MacEwen refers to the techniques reminiscent of southern US American bluesmen and about Rolling Stones lead guitar player Keith Richards, who studied those same American musicians and whose adaptations made the Stones's music stand out from every other major rock group, the song "Satisfaction" being an example.

"Gene wove these intricate and ancient chords into his melodies, which no one else was doing, and it gave his songs a memorable quality that made you want to sing along," says MacEwen. "Think 'Put Your Hand In The Hand.'"

He believes that Reno understood how Gene could use these techniques and could articulate loneliness into a song and convey what he referred to as "a deep-felt love.

"Gene had a deep well of feeling," says MacEwen. "Not everyone can write songs the world will love, but Gene's music was a ministry of love that communicates strongly with the listener. He was a man of mystery. He was a man of ministry. He was a man you don't meet every day."

MacEwen says that Catherine is not only "the spitting image of her dad" but that she also shares the same innate musical sensibilities.

"This is something to witness, greatness continuing its journey. I believe they share one tight spiritual connection; Gene saw music as a ministry of love, and I believe Catherine does too."

⚮   ⚮   ⚮

Gene and Reno did *The Tommy Hunter Show* and the two other commitments and before they knew it ended upon on a national Canadian tour with the Canadian pop music band The Bells, performing all the way from Vancouver to the Maritimes. Following that tour, they found themselves at the Canadian National Exhibition following a performance by the US country-music legend Charlie Pride.

"I think he had like a twelve-piece-band, with a whole string section and the works," recalls Reno. "They were a real great band."

What followed was nothing short of comedic.

"Gene and I got onstage after Charlie, and the wind was blowing, and we only had the two microphones. They were swaying back and forth, and Gene said to the audience, 'I'll introduce you to my twelve-piece band here.' But he just had his little guitar and there we were, playing away."

The Tommy Hunter Show, the Bells engagement, and the CNE engagement all took time. But they had the mutual presence of mind to get back to where their hearts and their spiritually were leading them. Gene had returned to Toronto, Reno was on the Island, but within less than a year, Gene contacted Reno and asked if he wanted to share the recording of an album with him.

"He said, 'I don't have enough songs,'" recalls Reno. "'You'll do half and I'll do half.'"

jack mcandrew
vice-president
gene maclellan
secretary-treasurer and
ronald dalzell

MACLELLAN/BELLS TOUR — PRELIMINARY ITINERARY

RUARY 16 .... TRAVEL TO TORONTO

RUARY 17 .... TRAVEL TO LONDON, ONTARIO

RUARY 18 .... CONCERT LONDON

RUARY 19 .... TRAVEL TO KITCHENER/CONCERT

RUARY 20 .... TRAVEL TO SUDBURY/CONCERT

RUARY 21 .... RETURN TO TORONTO

RUARY 22 .... PROMOTION IN TORONTO

RUARY 23 .... PROMOTION IN TORONTO

RUARY 24 .... PROMOTION IN TORONTO

RUARY 25 .... PROMOTION IN TORONTO

RUARY 26 .... CONCERT IN TORONTO/MASSEY HALL

RUARY 27 .... TRAVEL TO KENORA/CONCERT

RUARY 28 .... TRAVEL TO DRYDEN, ONTARIO/CONCERT

RUARY 29 .... TRAVEL TO BRANDON, MANITOBA/CONCERT

:H 1 .... OFF DAY OR TRAVEL

:H 2 .... EDMONTON

:H 3 .... REGINA

:H 4 .... CALGARY

:H 5 .... SASKATOON

:H 6 .... LETHBRIDGE

:H 7 .... VANCOUVER

:H 8 .... VICTORIA

:H 9 .... PORT ALBERNI

NOTE: CONCERTS

DAYS NOT

IN THIS O

A preliminary itinerary for a MacLellan/Bells tour.

Reno took his family to join the MacLellans, all of them living in one house together in Burlington, Ontario, while the album was being recorded, and then when the two men set out on a newly themed cross-country sojourn.

"We did a lot of hospitals, charity things, and whenever we were asked to go and play, it had nothing to do with getting paid as much as going and just singing the message 'Jesus loves you.'"

They didn't care where they were playing or if it was a church, for what denomination, as long as they were delivering their message.

"I had never been in the devotion," [quite the way Gene was], says Reno, "but when I was a little boy, I'd always had a belief. I'd always leaned towards that."

Reno was brought up Roman Catholic, served as an altar boy, and there were serious family and local parish-priest expectations that he would go into the priesthood or brotherhood. But the hypocrisy of the church created a distance between him and Catholicism, he says.

"Everybody would be fine on Sundays but on Mondays, they would be doing the same bad things they'd been doing. So, I lost interest in going to church."

He searched everywhere to find the answer, looking through all different religions, finally coming across something that he read in a book that told Reno: "Go back to the beginning. You'll never find the truth unless you go back to where you really came from."

"So I started to read the Bible and I got to Ecclesiastics and a verse in there sent me right to the gospels of Christ and that was my answer. I had all the answers I needed. I had no need to ask anymore."

Throughout their travels, Gene and Reno could sense which people were true believers versus the hypocrites. They had discovered something wonderful together: the truth.

It was tough being on the road so much, but the gratification of living out their beliefs and the assurance of having families at home gave them an odd kind of stability.

"We were always lonesome when we were out on the road playing and glad to be doing it because we were bringing our heart's message to everybody.

But when it came time to come home to be with the kids, that was the best part of our lives. I've never seen him happier on the whole thing than the day we were going home.

"He loved his family so much. Whenever we were on the road doing things, it was just, 'When are we getting home. When are we getting home?' The best part of the whole trip was always the coming home part. His children just meant so much to him, and his wife, of course. He was always really excited and exhilarated to get back home."

Two of those people Gene and Reno were, at times, getting back home to were Catherine and another Island singer-songwriter and performer: Reno's daughter Tara MacLean, who feels a deep kinship with the MacLellans. MacLean's parentage is a complicated sidebar to the Reno-MacLellan story, a sidebar with three main characters.

"Marty was there with me when I was born," says MacLean. "My mom was pregnant, and I was born, and he raised me and taught me everything I know about music, and yet my mom, actress and singer Sharlene MacLean, says there is a very good possibility that my actual father may be someone else—my biological father."

That other possibility is Danny Costain, a singer and a dancer who spent time with the Charlottetown Festival musical theatre company, the same company which saw Sharlene appear at different times in her career as young Prissy Andrews and later as Mrs. Pye in the longest running musical in Canadian history, *Anne of Green Gables*. Costain and Sharlene were together for five years before she met Reno.

"So basically, the deal is that both of these men claim me as their child," explains MacLean. "So I have two dads. End of story."

With all three parents as music and performing-arts professionals, it was inevitable that MacLean would continue in the industry.

"Catherine is a really close friend of mine," says MacLean, "more like a sister really, because we kind of consider our fathers to have been brothers. We just have this incredible history with our families so we are very, very bonded that way. I just think the world of her. She is one of the most incredible women I know."

Because Gene and Reno were so close for twenty years, it means the world to MacLean that she and Catherine have found their closeness together. And it extends throughout the family. Catherine's brother, Philip, was the engineer on MacLean's record, which allowed them the time and space to rekindle their friendship too.

"And [Catherine's mother] Judy loved me and came out here to visit and hung out with my children. We are just a family, and the fact that music has connected us is everything. There is a lot of love here. That's all we could ever ask for because that's all anyone is really looking for in life is love. That's what we are doing here and there is a lot of love in this situation."

MacLean and Catherine are on the same page about one another.

"It's funny," says Catherine. "We've known each other all these years and felt like family, but since we've been doing similar things musically and spent more time together, it's been lovely. I do feel close. Like sisters just really getting to know each other."

MacLean feels that they've learned to love because they had a lot of love from their fathers.

At the time the Renos and MacLellans were living together in Burlington, Catherine's brother, Philip, was MacLean's age, so they were good friends. Catherine's sister, Rachel, was MacLean's sister Shay's age.

"Catherine was in Judy's belly," says MacLean, who was born in 1973, "so I didn't even get to know her except briefly as a baby. I didn't really know her until I guess it was probably her late teens," because Gene and Reno kept working and touring together.

At the time they truly connected, Catherine was just starting to play music professionally.

"I had already spent years as a professional musician and had signed with a label. When I heard her songs, I just was completely floored. I realized that she had the gift and so we connected. I basically got all of her albums to make sure that I had heard every single thing she had written and I listened to them constantly. It made me feel, I don't know, there was this incredible legacy being passed down. I mean, Gene's music was such a big part of my life, and his and Marty's music together was the big reason why I became a songwriter and a singer and guitar player," directions having nothing to do with the fact that she was once destined to be a lawyer.

"I mean, why would I want to be a musician?" poses MacLean. "That's so unstable. You know, I love the arts, but I was sort of like the oldest child and thought that I should probably do something that brought in money and that had some kind of stability. And no matter how much I tried to run away, it just kept following me, and it turned out that I was a strong musician and I decided to do that. But it was always like I'll make one more record and then make one more album and then I'm going back to school."

MacLean talks about the fact she was so heavily influenced by Gene and Reno. But later, hearing Catherine's music was also profound.

"Hearing her music was like hearing music that was familiar to me in a way that no one else's music could be."

MacLean has been living in western Canada since she was roughly thirteen. But she and Catherine are always trying to connect. With MacLean settled into British Columbia and Catherine at home on the Island, the best they can do is get together as often as possible when MacLean gets home to the Island.

MacLean and her husband, Ted Grand, live on Salt Spring Island, from where he oversees more than seventy Moksha Yoga studios around the world.

MacLean recently recorded an album, which she chose to lay down at Catherine's Dixon Road studio with Gauthier. Cutting the recordings in a studio adjacent to Catherine's house gave them a lot of quality time together. MacLean asked Catherine to join her production, *Atlantic Blue*, at the Guild in Charlottetown as a guest performer. And their kids are friends. Catherine, of course, has Isabel and MacLean has three girls who are nine, eleven, and fifteen years of age.

"So there is a third generation of connection there, and we made sure to foster that relationship. We go to the beach together, and the most important thing is that we really, really support one other in our dreams."

That applies to playing music but also having healthy family lives. MacLean says that that is one area where neither of her or Catherine's parents were very good at—finding a balance. Reno and Gene would be on the road a lot, so that was a factor.

"So we are trying to sort of create a different atmosphere. It is the number one priority," according to MacLean, who adds that both she and Catherine discovered early on, and believe more than ever today, that they can use music as a way to live and how "to navigate the rough waters of life."

She talks about both Gene and Reno as having influenced both of them through their music, starting from the time she and Catherine were small children. Music became an integral part of who they are, how they see themselves, and how they see the world.

"I have the same feeling with Gene in a way because you know, he approached things from a way songwriting-wise that although there was sadness in it, there was great poetry and it was always looking for something bigger, something greater than himself to help move him through, whether he called it love or God."

MacLean says Catherine has shared deeply with her about her experiences, about her life, about her father and his influences, and his passing.

"That means a great deal to me because Gene was so fundamental to my becoming who I am. Gene was as much like an uncle as anyone ever could be and I would sit and listen to he and Marty play music together for hours. That is how they communicated with each other. Getting to be there when music was either happening or being created was fundamental."

MacLean was drawn into their music at a very early age, before Catherine was born. On one of Gene and Reno's albums, she was included as a background singer for a song called "Mommy." She was only four or five at the time.

"I remember sitting there and singing and just having this incredible experience of being part of this song," MacLean reminisces. "That was my very first recording experience."

Gene was there at Christmas, she recalls.

"He would buy us beautiful gifts. I actually spent a Christmas with Catherine when she was very small one year in Burlington. I remember Gene sneaking into the room to give us our stockings and I woke up and he was putting the stocking by the bed. I was like, 'Gene was Santa!'

"Then I remember him teaching me how to like draw butterflies and cut them out of paper. I just have lovely hands-on visceral memories. But my greatest memories are of his voice and of him, you know, of him singing and being in the room with him and his face and the way he would move his body when he was playing, like the way he would move his shoulders."

MacLean talks about how every musician moves in their own unique way when they're playing and singing. Some artists are still and some are very animated. She recalls Gene closing his eyes and losing himself in his music.

"When he and Marty would be going, it was like...euphoria for them. I still can see his sort of sideways smile and just, you know, moving his head, his hands, and tapping his foot. I can just see the whole thing. It is really clear to me."

MacLean talks about being not just a fan of Gene's, but of Catherine's.

"I love that I get to love her as my family but I also get to love her as an artist. And she is also so different than Gene in a lot of ways. She is less religious. She is really her own songwriter and her own creator in so many ways, but still reaching for that higher ground."

MacLean says it's a matter of semantics. For Gene and Reno, it was about religion. For Catherine and for MacLean, it is spiritual, lyrical, and descriptive.

One of the ways MacLean connects through Catherine and her music involves how Catherine approaches sadness differently than her father did, something that she very admits is hard to describe. Still she views Catherine as having a higher mastery of it.

"I mean, she's a woman. She's in a completely different time than her father. She's quite emotionally and incredibly aware and strong. She's phenomenal.

"These fathers of ours gave us tools for survival. Without knowing how to write a song, I don't know that we would survive....The reason that Catherine is great is because she writes to live. I mean that in the sense that like life wouldn't be complete without it."

It is their mutual therapy.

MacLean's view of God is closer to Catherine's view on religion than to either Gene's or Marty's or her mother Sharlene's. She leans more toward a Buddhist way of living. And like Catherine, she got a healthy enough exposure to traditional religion early on in her upbringing. Sharlene was the Sunday school teacher where they attended church as a family.

"Not religious. Just more of a way of being. I think that you know that Jesus was a great teacher and a rebel and amazing, and I am really grateful that I got those teachings as a child. I am just not into the fundamentalist organized religion."

The practising of religion aside, some of her fondest memories are of travelling around to different churches and singing as a family.

"That was sort of our way, including sometimes that was how we got money. Marty was just so involved in the church and they would testify about how they came to God. In a lot ways, the church really helped them. And in the end, I have different view of how to move through life because I'm just not a literalist. I don't take the Bible literally."

MacLean refers to her and Catherine as "little Zen weeds" who connect deeply on the same life philosophies.

Land call us home
Let's gather round
Let's tell the stories that remind us
of where we're all from
Let's sing the songs that our parents sang
Bring us all together
With those family names

—"Family Names" by Catherine MacLellan

You and me we're not so different

Pilgrims in this world

Keeping our emotions in

Like frightened boys and girls

There go you...there go me

But for the grace of God

We never know where we might be

—Untitled, unpublished lyrics from Gene MacLellan's personal journals

CHAPTER 6

Out of the Shadows

Catherine is acutely aware that her father had a daunting alter ego—and we're not referring to his novel's protagonist, Willard. That other alter ego was his nemesis, depression, a cruel irony for a man who worked as an orderly in Prince Edward Island's psychiatric unit at the Hillsborough Hospital. No matter what else was going on, there were always shadows surrounding him, deep and pervasive shadows that sometimes held him hostage. The shadows projected a sense of loneliness. He was a man very much alone in life, following a solitary path even though he could be surrounded by family. Such is the isolation of depression.

Friend and fellow artist Lennie Gallant was among countless people who were devastated by Gene's suicide. Many felt they had more time they wanted to spend with this man who longed so much to be alone.

A few months before Gene died, Gallant talked to him on the phone about getting together, a prolonged commitment, which they both kept rescheduling.

I've been lonely like you, just
in case you've been wonderin
And I've been on the mountain-top
at times
I've been on fire and I've sometimes
been empty inside
But with ~~Heaven's the~~ help of ~~my~~ friends
I've always made it through
~~And this song's for you~~ JUST LIKE YOU

You and me we're not so different
Pilgrims in this world
Keeping our emotions in
Like frightened boys and girls

There go you... there go me
But for the grace of God ~~in Heaven~~
We never KNOW where we might be

I've been changing my mind like the tides
and the season
And I've been changin' the way
I look at you
You were there when I needed someone
to believe in me

CHANGES DEEP INSIDE LONG OVERDUE

They engaged in a series of backs-and-forths about commitments and "having the family today" and the typical demands of daily life.

Gallant remembers Gene asking him to call him back again.

"Don't worry, I will," responded Gallant.

Those few short months passed, and Gene was gone.

"Mental health is a big issue as a survivor of suicide," says Catherine, referring to herself as a survivor of her father's death. "Figuring out, why did that happen? Why did my dad die? And then realizing that I was suffering from depression and anxiety."

As it would be for anyone, Gene's death was the most traumatic experience of Catherine's life.

"In the period after we found him," according to Judith, "she went upstairs to her room and wrote some really nasty stuff."

Catherine was fourteen years old and in grade ten. She reacted by isolating herself and writing, posing questions like, "Why?" And other things like, "I hate you."

As Judith says, this was to be expected.

"I knew she was struggling, so I took her to see a child psychiatrist."

Judith knows that it was a bold but important decision to make at the time, ignoring the societal stigmas associated with mental illnesses, some of which continue to this day.

"Twenty years previous you wouldn't do it," she says of the decision to seek out professional help for her daughter.

Catherine went to that psychiatrist just the one time and adamantly refused to go back.

"This sums Catherine up," says Judith. "She went to see him once and said 'I'm never going back.'"

When Judith pressed her as to why, Catherine wouldn't tell her mother except to say that when Catherine asked *him* a question, he didn't answer her.

So Judith resigned herself to the fact that Catherine knew her own mind.

Catherine was not alone in the need to speak to someone.

"I went to see someone for a year or more after Gene passed," says Judith. "I said, 'I need help.'"

She needed and sometimes still needs someone to bounce her anger or frustration off.

Catherine says she more or less gave herself counselling to alleviate the anxieties and depression she was experiencing.

"I've gone to a few people, I guess, for just one session here and there. We were encouraged to go see someone," referring to herself and her mother, Judith, going together.

"I think she was pretty worried about me actually. It was just after Dad died. A couple months after. And the guy was very busy and he gave me a checklist, or the receptionist gave me a checklist."

Catherine recalls it as a ridiculous experience—being provided with a checklist of questions like, "How do I feel?"

"It was like a page long, and I just had to check all the boxes. Afterward, I went into his office. It was about twenty minutes long. He looked at the checklist. He said, 'How are you doing?'"

"Pretty good," she recalls saying.

"I was a kid. I didn't want to show my emotions to a stranger. And then he's like, 'Have a nice life,' basically. It was the worst thing, and from that point on, I never wanted to see anybody in that kind of way ever again. It's like 'what a waste of time.'"

Catherine felt like he simply did not care. She likens it to food poisoning and never wanting to go near the root cause, food, again.

"Instead, I just started talking to people about it within my friendship group in Summerside. I started doing yoga and a bit of meditation," which she still does some of today, the Shambhala Buddhist style which involves ten to fifteen to twenty minutes of sitting and contemplation at a time.

"I go through phases of it. I find that it really helps with my self-awareness and acknowledging when I am getting depressed and when I am in a moment of anxiety or panic. They still happen because it seems to be part of my makeup."

Of far greater help than the psychiatrist Judith took Catherine to was her adventure to the other side of the world. Two years after Gene's death, some aware teachers and other community people in Summerside thankfully stepped in to help save Catherine from her grief and seclusion.

Catherine was nominated as a candidate for a Rotary exchange program, which sent her to Australia at this, the most critical, time of her life. Gene, of course, was not exactly Rotarian material, so had never been a part of the worldwide Rotary or any other service-club scene. Candidates applied through their high school, answering questions such as, "What are you going to do after high school?"

"I just put my name down and I got to get away. I was chosen, I think, because they thought I needed to go away."

"They" were her teachers and people at Rotary in charge of the program. And they were right.

"I was a pretty shy, quiet kid who had been through a lot. All my teachers had witnessed me go through a lot in high school, and I think they just thought it would be good for me. And it was probably the biggest year of my life as far as change goes."

She doesn't recall being scared or intimidated by the challenges of being relocated at the age of seventeen.

"I think I was kind of numb from everything that had happened with Dad.

"I don't know why, but I was on autopilot. I think the shock of losing my dad and then kind of the grief that goes with it kind of just shut me down. It is a pretty hormonal time for girls, so I was still going through normal girls' teenage stuff, having boyfriends. I wasn't very present I'd say for most of those years."

She remembers how she felt leaving.

"I was kind of excited. I didn't really think anything of it. I didn't cry when I left. I am sure my mom was bawling her eyes out. Anyway, yeah, I was just kind of on autopilot, and then I got there and then I think that was a major piece of the healing for me, including figuring out who I was as a young adult. I turned eighteen there."

A teenage Gene with a guitar. (Courtesy of Ray Dart)

It meant she had to do an extra year of high school, but that didn't matter to her then or now reflecting back. It was Catherine's chance to break out of her bubble and she made great friends down under.

"I figured out who I was because I didn't have my family to hide behind or any friends. So I had to make friends."

Catherine met up with another twenty or so kids from Canada on exchange trips to Australia who'd been on common flights. But when they arrived in Australia, she remembers, the rest of them seemed headed for the Gold or Sunshine Coasts while she ended up being in a remote area of the country in the desert.

She was billeted over the year there with three different families—first with Cindy Diamond and her partner at the time, followed by the Taylor family and finally, the Oldmans. Dr. Oldman was one of Australia's flying doctors, part of the Royal Flying Doctor Service, working out of a desert station in Broken Hill, in New South Wales, seven hours north of Adelaide.

When she returned to Canada, she went to Dalhousie University in Halifax for one year, but that was the end of her formal education. Dalhousie had not exactly electrified her.

"I just sat in my room and wrote songs, and then I came home again. I wasn't interested in university."

University aside, that time in Halifax was, although different from her Australian experience, formative for Catherine.

"It was great. We were all kind of neighbours and we all hung out a lot and we would meet each other at the same places."

Catherine's best friend, Tanya Davis, who was already living in Halifax, was a part of this "co-op." She and Davis had become close friends when the MacLellans moved back from Ontario to Summerside and their two families were neighbours there. The two young girls shared their wild imaginations together. Davis, who is known for her spoken word poetry, years later served as Halifax's poet laureate.

"A lot of people just came over to my house," says Catherine. "We had a big kitchen in a house on the corner of Windsor and Charles. It is actually the same house that Lennie Gallant lived in when he moved to Halifax. The next time I ran into Lennie, he asked, 'So, did you ever find a place to live?' 'Yeah, I did. I'm living at this house on Windsor Street on the corner of Windsor and Charles' 'Oh my God,' responded Lennie. 'I lived in that house. What bedroom?'"

"We even had the same room!" Catherine now laughs.

✳   ✳   ✳

From serious ailments in his youth to ill health during adulthood, Gene was not blessed, as Catherine is, with vitality and a strong physical grounding. He was "very slight" for his five-foot eight-inch frame, according to Judith, who confirms that Gene had polio as a young child growing up in Val-d'Or,

Unlike her father, Catherine was blessed with good health in her childhood. (Photo by John Sylvester)

and at the age of nine or so had open-heart surgery to repair a hole in his heart. These in addition to what is frequently referred to as a life-altering automobile accident as a young adult.

"When he had first moved to PEI," says Catherine, "I think there was a car accident, and he went to like get well with my great aunt Marjorie, one of the aunts on my grandmother's side of the family."

According to New Brunswick–based author Bob Mersereau, a journalist who has probably done more research into Gene's life than anyone else, there were several erroneous articles over the years that said that Gene was severely injured in a car accident that also killed his father, Philip.

"Not true," says Mersereau. "Gene's father was killed in December 1985 outside of Saint John, New Brunswick," while believed to be returning home to PEI from a shopping trip in Maine. Mersereau has spent time trying to find the date of the car accident that Gene spoke about in PEI that laid him up for several weeks, believing it would have been sometime between 1966 and 1968.

"He mentioned a separated shoulder," says Mersereau, adding that despite numerous references to a very bad car accident around 1964 in articles and press releases, he has found no solid proof. The articles usually say Gene went to PEI to convalesce and decided to stay.

"He talked about coming in 1964 but never mentioned an accident," according to Mersereau. "His sister Joan doesn't recall one."

Mersereau chalks it all up to how a series of stories sometimes merge into one to make them more dramatic and easier to sell in a press release, as this was not an uncommon practice in the entertainment world. That, or the stories just got mis-told by one journalist and took on a life of their own, with Gene not bothering to correct them, and his manager/publicist Jack MacAndrew never bothering to ask him about it.

Then there is the story of Gene's iconic eye patch, which some publications have attributed to injuries caused in a car accident. According to Judith, the patch really came about because Don Messer, the legendary Maritime musician and television host, did not like the look of Gene's lazy eye.

"So he had wardrobe make the eye patch," she says.

Gene on *Singalong Jubilee*, which ran on CBC TV. (Courtesy of MacLellan family)

Gene, she says, never wore it after *Singalong Jubilee* and *Don Messer's Jubilee.*

Whatever the true or false nature of Gene's automobile accident, he compensated as best he could for any physical shortcomings through the most offbeat of obsessions for a white Anglo-Saxon Protestant from Val-d'Or. Gene loved tai chi, a practice which Catherine used to think was funny to watch. As she matured, she saw beyond the humour of tai chi to the spirituality of the practice. Tai chi was, for Gene, the preferred form of physical meditation.

Recognizing that she, like her father, is prone to depression is an important part of life's ongoing challenge.

Stemming from Catherine's time living in Halifax, when she was experiencing panic attacks and high levels of anxiety, she got help from a professional who was equipped with a variety of coping "tools." She recalls not being very self aware and having a lifestyle that exacerbated the situation—being on the road playing music, missing home, missing Isabel, or being at home with Isabel and not being able to do anything but be with and take care of her.

The most severe depression Catherine experienced came upon her eight or so years ago. The exact timeframe is grainy to her. It was before Chris Gauthier was in the picture and she had just split with her then boyfriend, Andy, who had returned to Ontario. That fall, she just could not get beyond what she was experiencing. She couldn't get off the couch, experiencing several weeks of not really being able to do anything except the basic functions, even though she had four-year-old Isabel to look after.

"It was the darkest time of my life," she says. "That's when I went to see somebody who really helped a lot, helping me process. It's funny because I went into her to say, 'I'm really depressed. I need your help.' And she said, 'Okay, what's going on in your life?' "

That practitioner's name is Rachael Roy, today listed on PEI under Optimum Health Counselling Service, and specializing in helping individuals suffering from post-traumatic stress disorder, trauma, depression, and anxiety.

Thankfully, unlike Catherine's early visit to a psychiatrist, there was no mundane, meaningless checklist of questions with boxes to check off.

"She talked to me," says Catherine.

She talked to Catherine about what was going on in her life at the time and previously, especially details having to do with men. The specialist mined her way through Catherine's split with Andy, with the events surrounding her husband, Al, leaving her when she was seven months pregnant, and why she had even chosen to be with that man in the first place. Eventually they got to the core question facing Catherine.

"Were there any other problems with men in your life before that?" she asked Catherine.

"Well, my dad killed himself when I was fourteen."

That response, of course, gave significant pause to the conversation. The specialist was trying to trace back Catherine's trauma and the root cause of her problems. Roy no longer wanted to just look at the fact that Catherine had just split with her boyfriend.

"She helped me walk through that day that my dad died and me finding him, and I'd never been able to look back on that day and get past a certain point. After processing that with this woman, that's when my whole life kind of changed. I began to heal that core wound. She's amazing."

Roy helped Catherine sharpen some of those previously mentioned "tools," including meditation. She says that since meeting Roy she's been "fired up" about working on herself.

Catherine is unsure about what degrees and levels of professional help Gene may or may not have had during his life. She is aware of one time when Gene's father took him all the way to London, England, to see a psychiatrist—a measure which Catherine considers an awfully long way to go for help. Seeing the psychiatrist was apparently the only reason Gene and his father had crossed the pond.

Perhaps going to the UK was intended to shield the fact that Gene was seeing a professional. This was when he was younger and before he'd started a family and during the time when poor mental health carried more of a stigma than it does today.

We're lovers, you and I
Looks like a classic case to me
I think about you all the time
And miss you constantly

(I LOVE YOU)

Sweet little painkiller. Thank you **LORD**
Have mercy ~~on me~~ upon me, forgive my abuse

If I ever get out of this storm

PUT A FEW OUT THERE and see if we
can get some holds on them.
Send ~~copy~~ of demo to Glen Campbell ✓
               and the Oakridge Boys ✓

~~done~~

Sometimes the pain's ~~too~~ great, so I have
a toke. Then I can almost relax.
There's never any such thing as total relaxation
except when you're sleeping.

"It seems like a pretty drastic thing to do," remarks Catherine, although she recalls some sort of discussion that Gene had not been getting the type of help he needed in Canada.

It's one of those questions she wishes she could ask her father. She doesn't recall anything about Gene seeing any other mental-health professionals when he'd grown into adulthood and started the family.

"I think he used religion as part of his therapy," she says. "And marijuana. He was definitely self-medicated."

Gene would have been happy about Justin Trudeau becoming prime minister and the April 2017 passage of laws involving degrees of legalizing marijuana.

Amazingly, Catherine has spent more and more time looking mental health straight in the eye and doing so in a very public way—onstage.

"Onstage, I've been talking a bit about mental health and depression, and people always respond to it. You know, because nobody talks about it. Not enough people talk about it, and so this woman heard a bit of that in one of my shows and she was organizing this conference and asked me to speak at it to tell my story. And I did.

"I have been talking a lot, doing speaking sessions. The first one I did was at a suicide-prevention and awareness conference in Berwick, Nova Scotia, a session that lasted about forty minutes, a combination of talking and playing in front of an audience of about one hundred and fifty people.

"Most of them were survivors of suicide or had attempted suicide themselves and all had a story to share, so it was really a safe place to do it."

It was a safe place to do it, but that doesn't mean it wasn't challenging.

"It was terrifying. It wasn't easy at all, but it was maybe transcendent, like it was a really important thing for me to be able to talk about it openly like that. I have done it a few more times, including one in Charlottetown,

In this story, Gene is described as "one of the most sought-after songwriters in the business, and his songs "a pungent mixture of loneliness and curiously old-fashioned themes."

Gene MacLellan

BY LARRY LE BLANC

At the beginning of the interview songwriter-singer Gene MacLellan seemed uncommonly reticent, almost embarrassed to talk about himself. It was partly because the open dialogue of an interview frequently violates his strict sense of privacy. As a rule, the slender, thin-lipped Prince Edward Island (Canada) resident keeps to himself and leaves the business aspect of a profitable career to Jack McAndrew, his manager.

Fed up by the increasing pressure and confusion of his success, MacLellan prefers the tranquility of his island home to one-night stands, big concerts and big-name television shows.

At 30-plus, MacLellan is one of the most sought after songwriters in the business. More and more performers, from Elvis Presley to Frankie Laine, consider it mandatory to have an ample supply of MacLellan songs in their repertoire. Songs such as "Snowbird" or "Put Your Hand in the Hand." He also is in demand as a performer, having received numerous offers to do lu-

crative concert and club dates. At present, however, MacLellan desires to more fully explore the area before fully committing himself as a performer.

Born in Val d'Or, Quebec, MacLellan grew up in Toronto. He played acoustic guitar before he was 10. And in his teens, he was a member of Little Caesar and the Consuls, a rock band. It was only because he was a budding writer, looking for new experiences, that he left home at 18. He worked as a busboy for more than a year in Rhode Island. Afterwards, he sang in churches and outdoor rallies across the country, ending up with a traveling evangelist called Bud Kena.

Eventually, he moved in with an aunt at Pownal, a hamlet about 10 miles east of Charlottetown. Trying to make a living, he picked apples and dug potatoes in the fall and worked as an attendant at the Riverside Psychiatric Hospital in 1966.

"My first break? I got booked on CBC's *Don Messer Show*," MacLellan recalled. "Of all the shows to get a shot on. It doesn't feature my kind of music. But the show certainly was a stepping stone."

After the Don Messer appearance, MacLellan joined country and western singer Hal Lonepine. The job lasted four months. He returned home to find an offer from CBC's *Singalong Jubilee* in Halifax. A sprinkle of outstanding local talent, including host Bill Langstroth, Anne Murray and Catherine McKinnon, was being featured weekly.

"Now Canadians are finding out there's just as much talent down in the maritime region as in Toronto or out West," MacLellan insisted. "Anne Murray proved it. I showed I could write. And there are a lot of writers in the area as good as I am, or better."

MacLellan loves the maritime landscape. In fact, everything about the area —from the cold cleanness of the air to the straightforward honesty of the people. He took great pleasure in bringing his wife, Claudia Mannion, a former Montreal art student, there to live.

Our talk turned to the creation of songs. Writing for MacLellan is a lot of hard work and exact planning. "I start out with a sound in my head," he explained. "Developing the melody is the easy part, in my case. I don't know how people like Leonard Cohen figure it out. He's a word man, a fantastic poet, who finds creating melodies difficult. Any way you look at it, though, the songwriting process isn't easy."

MacLellan's songs are a pungent mixture of loneliness and curiously old-fashioned themes, echoes of country music and more than a suggestion of a restless rock beat. When he interprets his own material, MacLellan's voice is mercifully free of the whiny self-pity that haunts most singers of love-torn lyrics. His phrasing and pronunciation on "The Call," for example, are not terribly different from what you might hear in the voices of George Hamilton IV, the Mercy Brothers or several other country-oriented singers. "I was brought up on country music," he admitted.

The songs, he agreed, are for himself, but he feels his best songs should be heard. "That was the initial thing when I started—I just wrote songs for myself. I enjoyed them. When they became community property I have to admit I was happy. It's nice to have your things accepted."

Mr. LeBlanc writes regularly for both Rolling Stone *and* Record World.

Courtesy of Canadian Broadcasting Corp.

another at UPEI, and another for the Department of Veterans Affairs. If some-body asks me, I'll do it."

In fact, the second act of Catherine's live tribute to her father at the PEI Brewing Company speaks eloquently to what he endured through his depression and what she and her family experienced through his suicide. This may sound like a downer for a night intended to uplift and entertain, but it somehow all works. The subject is crafted into the production without Catherine seeking empathy, and audiences respond with a clear message back to her—they are with her all the way and, more to the point, everyone in the room is experiencing or has experienced something very close to her narrative. Some without a doubt experience or have experienced depression themselves. Others are victims to suicide in their family or friendship structure. That Catherine was able to take herself there and back, night after night, speaks volumes to the strength she has mustered.

"It just tore me to pieces and put me back together again," says close friend Tara MacLean about Catherine's tribute show.

She simplifies how Catherine could do more than thirty shows with so much emphasis on her father, saying, "She's a pro."

Coincidentally, while Catherine was doing three shows a week, MacLean was across town at The Guild doing three performances a week of *Atlantic Blue*.

"We were really cheering each other on throughout the whole process."

MacLean says there are times when a performer has to dig down to find the right energy level to make a show go over.

"Sometimes you are like, 'How am I going to get up onstage because I am exhausted?' We were just like so, so tired, but there is an amazing thing that happens when you get onstage. Your tiredness goes away and it is you and the audience, and this magic happens, and this energy appears that you didn't know you had—this reservoir of power. Sometimes when you think you have the least to offer is when you have more to offer."

Some well-known Canadians have also been brave enough to open up about their personal mental-health challenges and have campaigned to fight the stigmas attached to the disease. Margaret Trudeau, former wife of prime minister Pierre Elliott Trudeau and mother of Prime Minister Justin Trudeau, and six-time Canadian Olympian Clara Hughes (speed skating and cycling), are the two celebrity Canadians associated with the cause.

Known for her interviews and public-speaking engagements on the subject, Margaret Trudeau talks about living in "a private hell" for years before being diagnosed with bipolar disorder, which made her think she had lost her mind. One of her primary challenges was feeling and being isolated to the point where she "really couldn't live." She has gone on to inspire countless Canadians through her public appearances and candour.

Hughes is the highly visible spokesperson for the Bell Canada "Let's Talk" mental-health services campaign, who has repeatedly stated publicly "the only reason I've shared my story is to take that tiny baby step of breaking down the stigma attached to depression."

Appearing on billboards, television, and print collateral, flashing her picture-perfect smile, Hughes can be credited with helping create a breakthrough on the subject. But, she admits that the picture-perfect smile is not necessarily her day-to-day reality, that she has relapsed into her disease, and that her battle is not over. There's no storybook Happily Ever After, even for someone able to perform and push through pressure and the physical pain of high-performance athletics.

✻   ✻   ✻

Judith is experiencing a high degree of gratification because of the way Catherine has tackled the issues surrounding Gene. She had always wished that more people could better understand him, that it "would inspire other people that may even be struggling with depression to just keep going."

"I hear so often Catherine talk about her dad now and how much he felt his love for them [Catherine and her siblings]. And I would agree with that. He loved them very much. He would have done anything for them. At the last, I know that when he ended his life, he was not thinking of anybody. Not even himself, as in most suicides."

Judith says that a lot of people think suicide is very selfish, but that they don't understand.

"I think a lot of people have tended to base their life impression of him on his depression and his battle with that. And I would like people to see a different side, because he inspired a lot of people, both onstage and through his one-on-one quiet generosity.

"There are musicians on the Island that he took aside and said 'Continue doing what you're doing,' or he went out and bought them a guitar because they didn't have a guitar and they wanted to play or their guitar was wrecked. So he would go out and buy a guitar and give it to that person. He did that all the time."

One such person was Island performer Scott Parsons. Judith says that Gene inspired him and that there were a lot of other people who remember Gene for his generosity and his willingness to help anybody.

"Until you've seen someone go through the pain before they actually end their life, you don't understand. And I think if you take that whole last six months of his life away and see what he would do for any of the kids, before he really got depressed to the point of where he wasn't functioning well. He would have done anything. And he did. Philip went to school to become a sound engineer and when he came home, they were going to build a studio."

She says that Gene had gone out and bought a huge soundboard.

"It was a big monstrosity that sat in the dining room," recalls Judith. "There was no dining room table. Just the soundboard."

Judith recalls an instance when Gene had to take Catherine to Charlottetown to see an orthodontist.

"It was like, you could see her eyes light up. 'Oh, great. I get to spend two hours with my dad.'

"I often wonder about all three children," says Judith, "especially Catherine because of what she is doing. I often wonder what their relationship would be like as adults. I would hope it would be a mentoring type relationship. I think he'd be the one to say, 'You know, go in a certain way,' but at the same time,

"So Little Take Me

Gene MacLellan's Snowbird *has* taken him places. Recordings of his song have sold more than a million copies and also

By Dick MacDonald

GREAT thunderin' Moses, the kilted chappie says, here's a surprise for ya . . . give a welcome to Gene MacLellan. Applause, much applause, and up to the stage shuffles an elf of a man, A-growin'.

Turtleneck sweater and sheepskin jacket, dark glasses partly hiding the consequences of polio and a car accident, he picks up a 12-string guitar. And can't think of a song. Well, why not the logical one, the one that indicated another Gordon Lightfoot is budding on the east coast.

A few chords strummed in the Charlottetown club and a Snowbird wings westward and northward and southward and just everywhere. More applause and cheers. Thank you, he says shyly, and moves into The Call and Face In The Mirror, two fine examples of his facility with bluesy ballads and country sentiment.

Vital statistics of a poet: Name, Gene MacLellan. Age, 31. Born, Val d'Or, Que. Height, five-eight or so. Weight, 130 pounds. Marital status,

so he moved in with an aunt at Pownal, a hamlet about 10 miles east of Charlottetown.

He picked apples and potatoes in the fall, drove a truck and generally did whatever was necessary to survive in a province where economic opportunity is anything but bountiful. He worked as an attendant at the Riverside psychiatric hospital in Charlottetown. Song-writing started in 1966. Widespread recognition started to creep his way in 1970, with special thanks to a half dozen people, but especially to a lass from Springhill, NS, named Anne Murray. The operative word is Snowbird.

It was only MacLellan's second composition, written four years ago, and inspired by an uncle one chilly PEI day. By now the song has sold well over a million copies in North America (it was even on the hit parade in Bangkok). It launched Anne Murray on a highway of major television appearances and helped promote her three albums, which until then had had reasonable sales but nothing exceptional. And it made Gene

This newspaper story describes Gene, then performing in a Charlottetown club, as five foot eight and one hundred and thirty pounds and dressed, as was the fashion of the day, in a sheepskin coat and a turtleneck sweater.

he wouldn't push it. He would say, 'Maybe this is what you need to look for,' rather than saying, 'If you do this you are going to get that.'"

As far as Gene and what he would say about Catherine and her music, Judith says simply, "He would be so proud of her."

This sentiment leaves Judith tear filled. She doesn't like to reflect on all of the things that Gene has missed out on, like the fact she has eight grandchildren now, five of them Philip's, Rachel's two, and Catherine's Isabel.

✻   ✻   ✻

Needless to say, Australia looms larger in Catherine's life than it does for other Canadian and international kids who've trended toward taking a gap year out of their lives to hitchhike or work their way on farms and other short-term jobs while experiencing the land down under. She has returned to Australia just once since her Rotary exchange days and would like to go back, but this time with her music.

"I really want to go," she says, and why wouldn't she, given the doors Australia opened for her and the healing it gave her?

"My friend Chloe runs a folk fest there, but all their folk fests are in their summer which are our holiday season here."

It would be a great way to get into the music scene there, but Christmas would be disrupted. With twelve-year-old Isabel to consider first, that is not going to happen, at least for now.

Catherine's space is such that if Australia is meant to happen, it is going to happen. She is perfectly able to wait and see what the world brings, just like most everything else in her life.

Gone too soon, gone too soon
Left with the harvest and the waning moon
They tried hard to save you but it couldn't be done
God was calling home his son.

—"Gone Too Soon" by Catherine MacLellan

PART II - MUSIC

Beyond the sunset, o blissful morning
When with our saviour, heaven is begun
Earth's toiling ended
O glorious dawning
Beyond the sunset
When day is done
Beyond the sunset
No clouds will gather
No storms will threaten
No fears annoy
O day of gladness
O day unending
Beyond the sunset
Eternal Joy

—"BEYOND THE SUNSET," UNPUBLISHED LYRICS FROM
GENE MACLELLAN'S PERSONAL JOURNALS

CHAPTER 7

You Come to Me

Lennie Gallant knew Gene long before he knew Catherine. They became pretty good friends during the last seven to eight years of Gene's life.

Before that, he'd known Gene and would run into him at the odd venue, like the way he knew Marty Reno and so many other musicians of their ilk, but it was during those latter years that their friendship became cemented.

In the lead up to the deepening of their friendship, during that time when Gene had more or less disappeared from the music scene, Eric MacEwen contacted Gallant saying Gene "was going to get back on the horse. He wanted to get back out there and play."

It was around 1989 or 1990 and Gallant was doing a big school reunion at the North Star Arena in North Rustico, PEI.

"I had my full band, and they were putting a lot of promo into it, and Eric asked, 'Can Gene come down and open for you?' I said to Eric, 'I can't have Gene MacLellan open for me. Are you crazy?'"

"Beyond The Sunset"

BEYOND THE SUNSET, O BLISSFUL MORNING
WHEN WITH OUR SAVIOR, HEAVEN IS BEGUN
EARTH'S TOILING ENDED, O GLORIOUS DAWNING
BEYOND THE SUNSET, WHEN DAY IS DONE

BEYOND THE SUNSET NO CLOUDS WILL GATHER
NO STORMS WILL THREATEN, NO FEARS ANNOY
O DAY OF GLADNESS, O DAY UNENDING
BEYOND THE SUNSET, ETERNAL JOY

A photo of a young Gene at the beginning of his music career. (Courtesy of Bud King)

Catherine MacLellan. (Photo by Oliver Tamagnini)

The Raven's Sun cover.

When not performing, Gene often dressed conservatively in sports jackets. (MacLellan family)

Catherine. (Photo by Rob Waymen)

The cover of *If It's Alright With You - The Songs of Gene MacLellan* by Catherine MacLellan.

Catherine MacLellan

IF IT'S
ALRIGHT
with you

THE SONGS OF GENE MACLELLAN

"Catherine MacLellan is a talent in her own right, surrounded by a great supporting band, but the real specialness of this show is that they all possess the maturity to allow themselves to be momentarily subsumed and lifted by Gene MacLellan's spirit. And that is a special act of generosity well worth witnessing."

COLM MAGNER, THE GUARDIAN

catherinemaclellan.com

CATHERINEMACLELLAN.COM

A promotional poster for Catherine.

Catherine with her partner, Chris Gauthier. (Photo by John Sylvester)

Catherine. (Photo by Jule Malet-Veale)

But Gallant said he would love to have Gene join the show as a special guest if he would come. Eric said that that would be great. Gene had started going to Gallant's shows and apparently had taken Catherine, at the time very young, with him.

"She told me later she used to come to my shows with her dad. And that meant so much to me, knowing that Gene MacLellan was in the audience, because when I'd started writing songs, I remember seeing this guy on TV on *Singalong Jubilee* who was this slightly dangerous dude with the eye patch. I remember being fascinated by him and his songs; it really made him a serious character and that intrigued me. He was a little bit different than other folksingers or other songwriters that were out there. I learned quite a few of his songs long before I knew him."

In preparation for the North Star Arena show, Gallant took his violin player at the time and went to see Gene at his studio in Granville to go over the MacLellan songs that they were going to do and to frame up how Gene would fit into the evening.

"We had a great rehearsal and had some fun there," recalls Gallant.

Gene asked Gallant what time he should be there and Gallant said 4:30 would be a good time to do a sound check. Gallant says their conversation went like this:

"I'll be there at 3:00," Gene said.

"Well, 3:00 is good, but 4:30 is when I need you there," Gallant replied.

"I'll be there at 3:30," said Gene.

"Well, 3:30 is fine too, but we are going to need you at 4:30," responded Gallant.

"Okay, well I'll be there before 4:00."

"OK. Good."

"We did our sound check," Gallant explains, "and 4:30 rolls around. No Gene. 5:00. 5:30, no Gene. 6:00, no Gene."

By then, Gallant, his band, and crew had to go have dinner and shower and get ready for the show.

"We were packing up and driving out of the parking lot and in drives Gene."

"Oh Jesus, Gene, where were you?' asked Gallant.

"Was I supposed to be here earlier?" asked Gene.

"You were supposed to be here at 4:00."

"Oh, I'm sorry."

Despite the time, Gallant, with his sound guy halfway out the door and wanting to grab a bite to eat, went back into the arena and did a quick sound check for Gene.

"That night when I called him up onstage halfway through the show to do a special set, the audience was excited. Gene started playing. I'll always remember his voice just going out in the back of the hall and coming back and bringing everybody with him. There was something so special about his voice, the way that it went out there and came back. I was kind of in awe at the way he sounded. I remember thinking, 'Gene MacLellan doesn't need a sound check. He just has that thing, you know.'

"I'll remember that night how his voice just carried so well. It wasn't a big voice; it just had a purity to it."

Gallant says that both Gene and Catherine possess a very sort of laid-back, yet very confident approach to their music.

Years later and after Gene's passing, Gallant recalls going to see how Gene's daughter was doing, to hear Catherine perform at downtown Charlottetown's Baba's Lounge.

"I remember the first song I heard Catherine singing there, with her voice coming out and doing that same thing. I said, 'Oh my God, she has that same quality in her voice that Gene had.' There was just something so inviting about it and so pure that it just went out there, bounced off the back wall, came back to us, and it took everybody's heart back with it when it came back. It was just really special.

"It's like, you are coming to me when I am singing my songs, and because, you know, if you really listen, you will connect to them. I think that is the way Gene approached his music."

Gallant believes that both just deliver their songs the way they were writ-ten, what he calls "being soulful with the song."

"If you are meant to hear it, you come to the song. You come to me. 'I'm not pushing this. I am inviting you. You come and experience my work and my words and melody.' I think that's the most spiritual connection between them and something he passed onto her for sure."

✳   ✳   ✳

Although the two became pretty good friends, Gallant was somewhat in awe of Gene. It was a thrill for Gallant to have Gene sit in the audience at some of his shows, after which they would go to Gallant's folks' place where "we'd have a great yack."

Gallant's folks were tickled to have Gene there.

"I remember one time, there was a famous bootlegger's place in North Rustico—Davey's at the Harbour, it was called."

It was one of the most notorious bootleggers on the Island, according to Gallant.

"There were many, many stories about Davey's—I could go on and on. We always went down there after our hockey games, and we would get served quite well. I remember when Davey, the elder, eventually shut the place down, and Davey, his son, hadn't opened it up again yet, which he did later. There was period of time when that bootlegger joint was inactive. And Eric MacEwen arranged a jam session at the bootleg joint when it wasn't active. It was nothing fancy, just an empty shed."

The jam was in the middle of winter, with a number of musicians join-ing Gallant and Gene as they passed the guitar back and forth playing and singing songs.

"That was so special to me."

But what Gallant remembers most about that night was Gene singing his new song "Puerta Vallarta" for the first time. He had just written it, accord-ing to Gallant.

"I heard it and I was like, 'Gene, man, what a beautiful song.' He said, 'Yeah, I kind of like that.' I was so in awe of Gene and I'll always remember he looked at me and he said, 'Do you have any idea how I could get someone to listen to that?' My jaw just about dropped to the floor, I was like, 'You're Gene MacLellan. You're asking me how you can get someone to listen to one of your songs?'"

Gallant can't get over the irony of it. Here was this man whose "Put Your Hand in the Hand" was one of the most recorded songs of all time, covered by legendary stars like Elvis, Andy Williams, and Bing Crosby, and he was wondering how he could get somebody to listen to his song.

Gallant talks about what it's like to perform "Put Your Hand in the Hand."

"It is such a classic. It is such a well-put-together piece of writing. I think that's what drew me to Gene's work to begin with. There are only so many songwriters out there that are so precise and economical with their words… and (it) just comes off like a beautifully crafted moment in time like a painting. And Gene was one of those people who had that great gift, you know. I loved all of them. They're all great songs. He didn't write any bad songs, I don't think.

"It is interesting that I've done some work down in Nashville over the years and every now and then, Gene's name would come up," says Gallant. "People would kind of take a breath and say, 'Yeah, whatever happened to that guy? Where is that guy?' People know him; they know his name. There was always a bit of a mystery, like, 'Where is that guy?'"

⚹   ⚹   ⚹

In spite of his legacy, several people attest that humility was a dominant part of Gene's personality; it's as though he never grasped the degree to which he was for many a household name or what he had achieved.

Eric MacEwen knows exactly how far Gene reached, calling Anne Murray's release of "Snowbird" a pivotal moment for Atlantic Canada and Canadian music.

"Gene's ascendancy to stardom with the success of 'Snowbird' marked the first time a songwriter from Canada's East Coast achieved such worldly status," says MacEwen.

Gene's turned out to an inspirational story for all aspiring songwriters from the region and across the country. Gene and "Snowbird" led the way in many respects, alongside the works of Gordon Lightfoot, for example. He transcended the boundaries that existed before the song was written. MacEwen still marvels at the fact that "Snowbird" was recorded in twenty-seven languages around the world.

"I heard it sung in Spanish in Madrid and in Italian in Naples," recalls MacEwen. "I can't express to you what it did for a creative soul from the East Coast. It was unbelievable. It made us believe we could do anything. It gave us a confidence we previously didn't have. And the fact that Gene was so humble was not lost on us. After all, it was the East Coast way—to remain humble through it all."

MacEwen tells the story of Cape Breton singer-songwriter Jimmy Rankin walking as a boy with his brother, John Morris, behind their three sisters, Raylene, Heather, and Cookie, on their way to school on a warm spring morning in Mabou. "Snowbird" was being heard on every radio in the world, and here were the Rankin sisters long before they were The Rankin Sisters, skipping along in the morning sunshine singing "Snowbird" with their naturally beautiful harmonies.

According to MacEwen, John Morris told his brother, "If you're going to be a songwriter, Jimmy, be like Gene MacLellan. Be the real deal, 'cause Gene MacLellan is the real deal."

"Gene inspired so many of us," says MacEwen, "Rita MacNeil, Ron Hynes, Lennie Gallant, and so many others. And the fact that our sweet songbird, Anne Murray, had made her way into the hearts of the world was over the top. East Coast music was reborn then, and we were to emerge into the contemporary songwriting world."

Lennie Gallant remembers another jam, this one an insiders' remarkable night at the ECMAs in Halifax involving a small throng of Atlantic Canadian music luminaries.

"It would have been '93 or '94 something like that," recalls Gallant. "Gene was there. It was the year Stompin' Tom was there. There was one night a bunch of us ended up at a hotel passing the guitar around the room. I know Ron [Hynes] was there. Jody was there from the Thomas Trio. The room was packed. I know I am leaving people out and I hate to do that. But we just kept passing the guitar around. We were having a magic night in that little intimate scenario, Gene sharing his songs, everybody sharing songs back and forth. That was pretty special."

Cape Breton-born singer-songwriter and musician John Gracie, who bases himself in Halifax and in 1995 recorded a tribute album to Gene, was one of those inspired and an integral part of that rebirth.

"Not to blow my own horn or anything like that," says Gracie, "but it was a surprise to everyone that it was a great success. We were able to make some of our money back," which, as he acknowledges, has been rare in Atlantic Canadian circles. Yet again, it took a Gene MacLellan connection, as was the case with Anne Murray and others, to help raise the potential of an Atlantic Canada artist.

Gracie never had the privilege of seeing Gene perform live.

"I do remember, of course, his being on television and *Singalong Jubilee* and places like that, and there are some videos out there on YouTube taken by people when he was entertaining people at prisons. I found all kinds of stuff like that."

But in addition to the mainstream material available, which showcases Gene, Gracie unearthed recordings that friends of his gave him from archives they had from many years ago.

"I recorded 'Reunion' kind of as a Christmas tune, a Christian song Gene had penned. Gene was a believer." It was a song made familiar to Gracie years ago by somebody who knew Gene from New Brunswick when Gene was doing tours of the prisons there. The guy was a piano player from New Brunswick, whose name Gracie can't recall. Gracie was playing downstairs in a pub, and the piano player was playing upstairs in the lounge where Gracie used to take breaks and watch him play.

"We developed a friendship there. He taught me this song on a break. I went home and researched it and I ended up recording it."

It was one of Gracie's first among many recordings, and the song, in a funny twist of circumstance, would serve as the focal point of their only conversation.

"I only got to speak to Gene once," recalls Gracie. "We were sitting next to each other at the ECMAs in Halifax. It was the first year that they had it at the Rebecca Cohn. We were both presenters."

Gracie leaned over during a low spot in the show and introduced himself, telling Gene he had recorded one of his songs and confessing that he hadn't yet sent along any money for the rights.

"He looked at me and laughed and said, 'This one is on me.'"

The two had a series of small chats during that ECMA event.

"He was a great guy," says Gracie.

That single chance encounter, plus Gracie's reverence for Gene's body of work, combined for what felt like "a punch in the gut" when Gene died.

Read to me from the book of Paul
I can't say that I believe it all
I just want to hear your voice ringing out

—The Chorus from "Now and Then" by Catherine MacLellan

Willard: Can you find it in your heart to lend me a dollar

Pedestrian: What do you need the money for

Willard: I'm fresh out of dough and I ain't got the money to call her

—Unfinished novel about Willard from Gene MacLellan's personal journals

CHAPTER 8

In My Father's Words

For a man with such an overflowing vault of inspired lyrics, Gene MacLellan had a minimalist way with words. If you read instead of listen to his lyrics, you develop an appreciation for their sparseness and simplicity. He did not write in labyrinths.

It's also fascinating that Gene had begun to introduce his song lyrics into the narrative of his unfinished novel about his alter ego, Willard. As illustrated in the excerpt from Gene's personal journals that he stole from his own song, "The Call," with references to: "Can you find it in your heart to lend me a dollar" and "I'm fresh out of dough and I ain't got the money to call her."

According to Catherine, he was a man of few words. But whenever he did choose to "speak"—or to sing—people tended to listen. And when he spoke through his lyrics, he spoke with deep meaning.

"Gene was always writing," says Catherine, "and he was always editing.

"More than anything I feel like what I got to witness was the editing process and he was kind of working on a book of his own, so he would mostly sit in

Willard: Can you find it in your heart to lend me a dollar

Pedestrian: What do you need the money for

Willard: I'm fresh out of dough And I aint got the money to call her

(The pedestrian reaches into his pocket pulls out ~~a dollar bill~~ some change, ~~too~~ gives it to Willard and walks off stage with a smile

Willard: Thank You. (After the Pedestrian walks off, Willard ~~rushes~~ to the Phone on the corner puts some change in anddials Mary's number. The Phone Rings but ~~her~~ No one answers ~~Willard sits back down falls~~

Willard slumps to the ground with another long Exhale + his head in his hands. ~~Go to black~~

the living room and kind of work on it, and picking away at things. It was all written out. He had beautiful writing too."

So try to imagine how beautiful "Snowbird" might have looked and what a keeper it would be, all written out in Gene's longhand.

"Give me something to write about and I'll write you a song," he scrawled in one of those small journals Catherine has in her possession.

Words, of course, come from many places. Gene was in love with reading, especially when it came to authors like Charles Dickens and C. S. Lewis. He wasn't academic. Catherine thinks he may have finished grade ten at best. But that didn't stop him from being a strong reader and, in his own way, intellectual.

Catherine reflects that he wasn't anguished over not having finished school, as it was more common during his era for young guys to drop out. She believes he would have liked to have obtained his high school diploma, but it wasn't anything he obsessed over.

"He was a smart guy," she says, "but I don't know if he was the right kind of smart for school."

Rather than school smart, Catherine says he was observant smart.

"He loved reading," she says. "He loved that private world that you can go into, I think. And I imagine he read a lot when he was a kid stuck in the hospital for weeks at a time."

And beyond the lyrics, there is the incomplete novel based on the viewpoints of Willard.

Writing songs were Gene's therapy sessions—as they are in a sense for Catherine—where pain can be expressed freely and without inhibition. Mindfully aware of her genetic disposition, Catherine believes that her father "had felt more pain in life than any one person should and that it was his sensitivity to life that caused him such pain, but rewarded him with the gift of lyricism and melodic composition."

One of the most important but least noted things Gene ever did was write "Shilo Song." In fact, the original title of this book was the line from that song, "I want you so much to be happy."

I had imagined that that line was Gene speaking to Catherine. And without prompting from me, she confesses she used to think as much too.

But Judith says we were both wrong.

"He told me that it was a song that was given to him by God and it was God telling him that he wants Gene to be happy," says Judith, repeating a key line from the song: "You don't have to be a superstar."

I love you for what you are
You don't have to be a superstar
Shining on the silver screen

"He told me that it was a God-given song," says Judith. "And that's why it is my favourite."

And although there are so many, it is one of Catherine's too.

Reinforcing the significance of "Shilo Song," Kiah Welsh, a Toronto-based contributing journalist to the Canadian Broadcasting Corporation (CBC), quoted Catherine in a January 2017 piece: "There's so many songs and so many stories about why he wrote [the songs he did] or who it is about. But, the 'Shilo Song' always felt like he was writing it for us kids and it's a bit of a pep talk. Like, you don't have to be a superstar and it talks a bit about his vulnerability. And, it's just kind of an encouraging song and it's really sweet."

Whether written as a message to Catherine, or to her and her mother and siblings, or to Gene's God, it is very sweet and rewarding to any reader or listener.

Catherine actually performed it at her high school graduation in Summerside. Catherine's favourite Gene song sometimes depends on where she is and what's going on around her.

On a three-week tour of England and Germany, she was driving herself in a rental car.

"I didn't have very many things on my iPhone to listen to, but one of them was this collection of my dad's songs that somebody put together for me. And I just kept listening to them over and over, and every time it seemed there was a different one I was crazy about."

I'm sittin in a hotel room
Down in Puerto Vallarta
A Mexican town
Where the sun comes around every day
A small taste of Paradise
Under blue Spanish skies
Tell my what more can I say
With the right señorita
And mucho dinero I'd stay.

CHORUS:
AND PLAY MY GUITAR
MAYBE WRITE A SONG OF LOVE // OR TWO
AND ALWAYS BE WHERE YOU ARE
AND NEVER BE THE ONE WHO'S LONELY
                                    AND BLUE
WHEN DAY IS DONE WE WILL LINGER
                                    TOGETHER
AND DREAM A DREAM FOR TWO
IN PUERTO VALLARTA
WHERE I COULD BE HAPPY WITH YOU

Walkin' down the streets of town
See the smiles on the faces
Señors, señoritas all greet you with peace + good
                                                    WILL
I know it's not the promised land
But to this common man
Anything like it would do
And I'd be one step from Heaven
In Puerto Vallarta with you.

Like the one called "Waiting on a Miracle," she says, in which Gene writes about the devil's ability to read your lips and read your mind and the need for a miracle to keep things in line. It's one of those Gene songs that Judith would like Catherine to sing because she thinks she could do a really good job of it. It was only released by one person that Judith knows of, recorded on the Capitol label in 1975 by Quebec-born singer Suzanne Stevens.

Judith always thought the song was about her, but she was told it was about another family member or perhaps the two of them. She was disappointed it wasn't just her alone.

She is trying to convince Catherine to record it.

Like everything else to do with her relationship with her father and his music, the miracle has already been witnessed. Catherine will cross the bridge toward performing and recording "Waiting for a Miracle" if and when it feels right.

And if you would, dear, I might take you with me
Singing the songs of oceans and streams

    — "Left On My Own" by Catherine MacLellan

I could write a book on you

A chapter or two, maybe more

To describe the look of you

Could take maybe three or four

—Untitled, unpublished lyrics from Gene MacLellan's personal journals

CHAPTER 9

WHERE MELODY COMES FROM

ene was known to love joining friends at musical house parties around places like Summerside. Someone would inevitably ask him to "sing that bird song," soon to become the international hit tune showcasing the odd dichotomy of a lover's pain juxtaposed against lilting, happy orchestrations, as though it was the ironic theme from some romantic comedy.

"People ask me to sing 'Snowbird' and I just don't sing like that, or I didn't," says Catherine, "and I was not interested in performing a hit song at my shows. I wasn't going to play it the way my dad did or Anne Murray or anyone else."

Catherine knows her dad did not sit down to write a hit song with "Snowbird" but that it simply came from within him based on what he'd felt one March morning while sitting on an old tree limb in a PEI field and watching a flock of snowbirds flitting in the air. He wrote the song in twenty-five minutes and could never explain it.

She says that Gene always sang it live the way you hear him sing it on his recordings, which is uptempo, the way Murray recorded it.

Usually when Catherine sings it, she sings it in her own quiet voice.

"Everybody has their own unique voice," she says, "and it is just how you absorb the world and spit it back out. That's how I think of it."

Catherine does two renditions of the song in her live tribute to Gene. At the top of the show, she accompanies herself on piano in a deeply quiet version, throughout which you could hear a pin drop from any table in the house. But she knows what the audience wants and needs, so she ends the show with a fun, uptempo version more in keeping with the Murray recording, followed by the show's rousing, celebratory closer, "Put Your Hand in the Hand."

"We were trying to come up with some sort of medley, taking the leftover songs that didn't make it into the show," says Catherine.

But it didn't work, so she and music director John Connolly decided to give the audience what they wanted most, even though the two closing songs had already had their airtime earlier in the show.

"For me, singing 'Snowbird' in that like upbeat way is fun and kind of hilarious. Like I would never choose to sing it that way, but it makes sense at that point in the show because the finale is a celebration. And I hope people enjoy that. At that point we are just giving it. It is kind of our one kind of showbiz moment. That's a good showbiz moment. I'm doing that forever. It's like, 'Here's your medley!'"

Without over-analyzing it, it's clear that "Snowbird" is the melody most people relate to when they think of Gene, if not one of the songs people think of when they reflect on Canadian music in general. In 2005, it was voted by listeners as nineteenth out of the top fifty Canadian songs ever on the CBC Radio show *50 Tracks*, hosted by then-popular Jian Ghomeshi.

Beyond "that bird song," there were so many others, including that transient song, "Thorn in My Shoe;" that wine song, "Bidin' My Time;" and the choral, rousing, "Put Your Hand in the Hand." So many of his songs are favourites of Catherine's both to hear and to perform, compositions like "Won't Talk About Love," "Face in the Mirror," "Song for a Young Seagull," "The Call," "Shilo Song," and so on.

Writing songs is ethereal, whereas sewing a dress or crafting a quilt, as Catherine talked of before, or cutting an album, is tangible.

"Making an album is about the only thing in my life that's concrete. And even that's not concrete. So a sewing project or doing something with my hands is important. Gardening is another big thing. I just started to learn how to upholster. I upholstered that chair," she says, pointing to one of only a couple pieces of furniture in her front room. "It's not finished yet."

"It's a project, so I like to start it, and I end it usually within a few days.

"Music, on the other hand, just comes out of nowhere. It's never really done. You just decide that is as much as I'm going to do on it," which suggests that Catherine changes her songs to some degree over time.

And how she sings a song today may sound somewhat different five years from now.

"It would sound similar. It's not really static. It doesn't just stay the same. The vibe could change or the way I sing the lyrics could change. Sometimes even the lyrics might change slightly."

After releasing her debut album in 2004, Catherine earned immediate critical acclaim, labelled Critics Favourite New Discovery by *Penguin Eggs* magazine in 2008. Since then, she has toured internationally extensively, and her music has been a perennial fixture at the top of Canada's Roots Music charts, winning acclaim from international media including The *Austin Chronicle*, The *Boston Globe*, BBC Radio, *Maverick Magazine*, and *Q Magazine*. It is no surprise that she is a Juno award winner, three-time Canadian Folk Award Winner, two-time ECMA winner, and fifteen-time Music PEI award winner. Her award-winning release, *The Raven's Sun*, takes listeners further along Catherine's journey in song, delving deeper into the territories of life, death, and transformation, most or all of which connects somehow, somewhere, back to her father and their relationship.

Left on my own I might sail off forever
Spend all my days in the waves of a dream

— "Left On My Own" by Catherine MacLellan

Treasures above

That's what I've been searchin' for

Most of my life

In the back of my mind

Treasures of love

Something I just can't ignore

Sittin' in the (indistinguishable) taking
    spanish classes

Lookin' for an open door

—UNTITLED, UNPUBLISHED LYRICS FROM GENE MACLELLAN'S PERSONAL JOURNALS

CHAPTER 10

MELODIC MELANCHOLY

everal Atlantic Canada artists see parallels between Gene's and Catherine's musical styles and personas, among them John Gracie, whose 1995 Gene MacLellan tribute album gained considerable critical and commercial success.

Central to these Gene and Catherine parallels is the understated tone of their compositions, which nonetheless are emotional and profound. Much of Catherine's work runs even deeper than that of her father.

Gracie is aware of the deep-thinking nature of Gene's music, a characteristic he had to respect when approaching the tribute album by not trying to spin Gene's lyrics and melodies into something they were never intended to be. He uses the example of how Gene had an uncanny, perhaps incomparable, ability to take melancholy and turn it into something light and melodic, as with "Snowbird."

"'Snowbird' is definitely an anomaly. It's happy and sad all at once. Like the Pat Boone hit song 'Moody River' which skips along gleefully but tells the story of a man who goes to meet his lover at an old oak tree by a river, but finds that she has committed suicide. In spite of the song's bleak narrative, it features a simple piano hook that is desperately catchy while at the same time is sad and lonely."

Similarly, most renditions of "Snowbird," including the original Murray one, have a happy lilt that deceives the listener.

The thing Gracie always noticed about Gene was that he could write what to other people felt like a happy calm, citing, for example, songs like "The Call."

"When you really listen to it, there is an underlying melancholy there which is a magical marriage of lyrics and music. Gene was really good at that — writing a song that had different counterpoints written within the song. He could write a melancholy song that would actually make you feel good.

"They are all great songs. That's the reason I think I was attracted to Gene's music, and also the fact that there's not many people writing songs that have that magical tone to them.

"I am a person that doesn't believe in the supernatural at all," says Gracie. "I don't believe in the spiritual realm at all. I believe when we see beauty in the world and we recognize it, we are moved as human beings. To recognize beauty, whether it is a sunset or whatever it is, and I think that is the same thing we experience when we see movies that touch us and hear music that touches us. That's the kind of magic that Gene had that he wrote into most of his songs. I think a lot of people hear it and they don't really realize it has two messages."

He says most listeners are getting the melancholy and the happy feeling combined subliminally so they're not even aware of it.

Gracie says that during the research phase of his MacLellan tribute album, he encountered friends of Gene's from the *Singalong Jubilee* days, including band members George Hebert and Garth Proude, all of whom made observations about Gene's music and his depth.

And when Gracie sees Catherine perform, it reminds him of Gene.

"My impression is that she is a deep thinker and she's very philosophical and I think her father was like that too. I think that's where the depth of those songs came from."

LET IT BE A SOURCE OF
LET IT BE A REFUGE TO SOMEONE
IN DESPAIR
WHO'S LOST THEIR WAY TO PARADISE
LORD I WISH I WAS IN MEXICO
IN CUERNAVACA WHERE THE LIVIN' IS SLOW
JUST YOU AND ME ABOUT A MONTH OR SO
TWO GUITARS, A RENTED CAR, A SPANISH RADIO

Runnin round like a chicken with
~~it's head~~ TRYING TO BE FREE
~~That's not the way to be~~
~~And no rest in that kind of life~~
And there never can be

LET THIS SONG BE MY SACRIFICE
~~GIVE IT WINGS AND CAUSE IT TO FLY~~
CAUSE IT TO RISE TO THE PLACE
WHERE YOU ARE
AND MAKE IT A BLESSING

LET THIS SONG BE MY SACRIFICE
LET IT BE MY PRAYER   LET IT BE SOME
                      COMFORT TO SOME-
LET IT BE A BLESSING LOR   BODY OUT THERE
TO THOSE IN DESPAIR
GIVE IT WINGS
LET IT TAKE TO THE AIR

Gracie doesn't pretend to know Catherine well on a personal level.

"She doesn't remember this, but she was just a little girl when I met her. We were doing this project and I went over with [Catherine's brother] Philip. I had supper with him and his mother and the two girls.

"I've spoken to Catherine since then and we've shared the stage. We were at the songwriters' circle at Jamfest a few years back, stuff like that."

Whenever Gracie has seen Catherine perform, including having had the chance to share the stage with her, he can see the threads that bind them together stylistically

"She's a very deliberate and thoughtful person. She sings deliberate and thoughtful. She doesn't rush through a song."

✗   ✗   ✗

Eric MacEwen spent a lot of time with Gene, including one late winter's night in an old farmhouse near Belfast, PEI.

"I had come over from Cape Breton Island to spend some time with him. It was a Saturday night; we were sitting round an old kitchen table having a cup of tea, or maybe was it a beer. The details are sketchy, but I shall never forget that it was the first time Gene and I heard Don McLean singing 'Vincent.' 'Starry, starry night' came pouring sweetly over the airwaves, and Gene and I remained silent during the entire song, transfixed by its beauty."

When the song was over, Gene asked MacEwen why he thought van Gogh had taken his own life. After thinking for a moment, MacEwen confessed that he didn't know.

"Gene said: 'I think it was because of the frustration Vincent had in communicating the beauty of life all around him, which nobody saw.'"

Sitting there together listening to McLean is a moment MacEwen will never forget.

"As it turned out, cosmically I believe," says MacEwen, "I was asked by a production house in New York City to travel with Don McLean on the performance circuit and interview him and weave a radio special on his life and music for distribution around the US."

McLean told MacEwen that he had suffered from a childhood disease, a severe form of bronchitis. Gene had experienced a childhood affliction as well, a heart defect, according to MacEwen. Their parallel was that both spent an inordinate time at home or in the hospital as children.

"Don told me his mother, who was mad about art, would sit by his bedside and show him wonderful coffee-table books about the great artists, one of whom was Vincent van Gogh. Later in his life, Don was to write this tribute song to the life of Vincent which the world came to love and revere."

MacEwen arranged for Gene to join him on McLean's performance tour and to visit his rural home in Garrison, New York. As MacEwen put it, they "understandably" became fast friends.

Harkening to Gene's love of sitting around playing music with friends, McLean is of the same ilk. Performing in Nova Scotia for one of his countless sold-out concerts several years ago, he sang all of his mainstream hits, transitioning into a more intimate part of the show after saying, "I have fulfilled all of my obligations." Although he was superlative, it was clear that the repetition of performing his old standards wears thin on him. When the last of the obligations was complete—McLean's heartbreaking rendition of Roy Orbison's "Crying"—he gathered his band around in a casual, party-like half circle and embarked on half a set of folk tunes that he loves to do. Gene could have sat right in.

Spending time with the two artists inspired MacEwen.

"The realization for me was that these two superlative songwriters had both emerged from childhood sicknesses to become known worldwide. Both Gene and Don helped me immeasurably in my career because of their determination to overcome disadvantages and to excel."

Let this song be my sacrifice
Let it be my prayer
Let it be a blessing lord
To those in despair
Give it wings
Let it take to the air

—Untitled, unpublished lyrics from Gene MacLellan's personal journals

CHAPTER 11

WAYS OF A SONGWRITER

Catherine talks intimately about her own finest work—its origins, parallels to her father's work, and its meaning: songs like "The Raven's Sun," "Rushing Winding Wind," "Sparrows," "Isabel's Song," "Now and Then," and more.

"I started writing after my dad died, and it was a very private thing," says Catherine. "Then I just spent a lot of time in my bedroom. Ever since, I've never had a feeling of lack of inspiration. There is always something to write about. I generally sit down with my guitar and a page of my book and a pen, and it just kind of flows out.

"I don't generally sit down with the idea of like I am going to write a song about 'this.' It is more like, I am feeling like there is something that wants to come out and I strum a chord on the guitar and play around with a riff or whatever until I feel like that matches the inner feeling, and then they kind of come out together. They come out at the same time. It's like the melody is very dependent on what the lyric is and vice versa, I guess."

It's like the words and the music coalesce in some middle space.

Catherine's favourite song is usually the one she's just written. At the time of our first interviews during the summer of 2016, that song was "I've Been Waiting On My Love."

"It's kind of a happy song," she says, about living in the present and knowing that everyone's time is short, so it's about "acknowledging the people that we love, and being there with them."

Catherine talks about how she has found a rewarding place through composing music, a mysterious place where vision, dreams, ideas, and emotion converge in her life. It's a similar, although not as dramatic a sentiment as expressed by her friend Tara MacLean, who talked about writing songs as a form of personal survival.

It's impossible to unravel the mystery of where songs come from, about the inexplicable art of finding and creating elusive melodies, and how it is a rare attribute she has the good fortune to share with her father. She agrees with the sentiment of the late Canadian icon Leonard Cohen, who liked to say that if he knew where songs come from he'd go there more often, places like the PEI field where Gene discovered "Snowbird" one day.

The mystery remains, the strange explanation of art, which Catherine grows more comfortable, familiar, and accustomed to, with every passing day.

Shaded in the background of Catherine's writing inspirations are several musical heroes, a list which always begins with her dad, but she is also attached to other artists, mostly from that same era, figures like Joni Mitchell, Bob Dylan, Cohen, and Neil Young.

"Those people influenced me probably more than anybody. Joni Mitchell would be at the top, the way she can write something really emotional and feels very personal but isn't necessarily about her. Just the way she writes is so creative and she's telling a story. It doesn't feel like a diary, although sometimes it does, but not in that soppy way of like in the '90s women's diary writing.

"I just happen right now to be on another Joni Mitchell kick, as always," she says. "There is this Michael Neil and Devon Spurle album that is more kind of indie pop. That really gets me going. I listen to Old Man Luedecke a lot. When he comes up, he is the first person when I plug my phone in and music automatically starts in the car.

"He's a great person. He's amazing. I love him. He was part of the scene when I was living in Halifax the last time. There was him, me, Jenn Grant, Rose Cousins, David Myles, Amelia Curran, and my best friend, poet and songwriter Tanya Davis, and we were all just kind of starting our careers. We were all just starting to tour for the first time, and making music our living."

✕ ✕ ✕

"I was born to do this, and my father taught me the ways of a songwriter," says Catherine. "I picked up music in the same way that a carpenter's son learns the trade. He passed it on."

Catherine says she first used songwriting as a way to find out who she was. "Now with every song, I hope to find truth in inspiration and light in the dark."

More of her music is deep and emotional than not. Rare exceptions to her serious musical subjects are a couple of country-like tunes she's created, including "Would You Marry Me For the Money, Honey" which started out because she and Gauthier always joke when they are really broke. The song is about a couple who get married so they can sell the gifts they receive. The other is a bit of a response song called "Bad Taste," essentially a breakup song.

"My friend Jack Marks wrote a song that it's like his girlfriend is asking 'how come you've never wrote a song for me?' And it goes on and on, and it ends up that this song with her complaining in it is the song he wrote for her and she doesn't like it, right? So, I kind of wrote a response to that which is like, 'you wrote one hundred songs for me, but none of them were true.'

"I can't live without you, or yeah, I've got this bad taste in my mouth basically from this relationship. I can't live without you, but maybe I can if I just spit you out."

✕ ✕ ✕

There is a certain sense of truth in Gene's and Catherine's songs. Reflecting on her father, she says that his sense of truth and honesty was a hallmark of his persona.

"He hated nothing more than a lie," she says, and that that principle carried itself into his compositions.

"I can tell you how I started playing music. It had a lot to do with my dad. I grew up surrounded by music. I was always interested in music. I sang in choirs. I played piano since I was six."

Catherine still has a piano and although she doesn't play much, she did open her PEI Brewing Company tribute to her father accompanying herself solo on the piano to a soft, slow, haunting rendition of "Snowbird."

"My dad was writing all the time. Friends coming to the house, jamming," she remembers. "People like Marty Reno, and we'd go to his buddy Tom's recording studio and I remember spending time there. Around that time I got my dad to show me the first few chords on the guitar when I was about ten and living on PEI."

Although she's left-handed, Catherine learned to play guitar right-handed on Gene's guitar.

"I'm not the only one though. It happens a lot if there is not a left-handed guitar available."

She can't play the other way.

"I tried actually, and I think I would have been a better guitar player if I had learned that way."

Interestingly, Catherine wasn't all that keen about getting Gene to teach her how to play the guitar.

"I wanted him to show me, and he wanted to show me, but it's very frustrating learning from a parent."

She had a guitar when she went to Australia and while there started writing more and more songs.

"I kind of became comfortable on my own playing songs. Not super comfy, but somewhat comfy. Just when we would get together with groups or at the school concert I did a song."

By the time Catherine performed "Shilo Song" for her high school gradu-ation, she was becoming more confident performing in public.

"I had played it on a few stages I guess at that point."

The first guitar she bought on her own was the second one she owned, a "crappy red Epiphone."

Today Catherine has so many guitars she has to stop and take stock, con-cluding that there are eight altogether, a lot of them cheaper guitars, but two (a Martin and a Collings) she considers performance quality, and a couple of Gene's are also "kicking around."

The Martin and the Collings, she says, sound like they are both brand new.

One of Gene's used to be her favourite instrument to play, but it was getting too fragile.

"Now it doesn't leave the case too much."

Being around so much music and learning to play piano helped lead Catherine into other forms of creativity.

"I'd always been very creative, writing bad poetry and stuff like that," she says, "and when Dad died, part of my grieving process was basically shutting myself in my bedroom and teaching myself guitar and writing all these sad songs. It wasn't a conscious decision. It wasn't like, 'This is how I am going to grieve.'"

She became obsessed with trying to use writing as a way to open up and communicate because she was so shy as a kid.

"I couldn't really talk to people at all, except for my closest friends. So I was able to communicate a bit of my sadness through music. And then people started getting me to play at things like a Lions Club benefit."

Breaking out of her shyness was definitely rooted in music. And in her dreams for herself.

"I just had this drive to play music so and, of course, one of my biggest daydreams as a kid was to be on the stage and for people to think it was good because I was so shy that I wasn't getting any feedback about how good I was at anything. All I wanted was for there to be this part of me that just wanted to say, 'Hey world! Here I am!'"

✻   ✻   ✻

Writing songs is such a challenging thing—the endless pursuit of something fresh and memorable and entertaining. Perhaps even more challenging is the art of co-writing, one of those rare artistic endeavours which many song-writers aspire to, but which few can successfully realize. It's an endeavour that Catherine doesn't spend a lot of time thinking about. What little she has done has been with several artists on PEI and in other parts of the Maritimes.

"I wrote one with Dave Gunning, which he put on his last record."

Catherine has, however, organized a songwriting group that meets every Tuesday during winter in Charlottetown and includes friends and fellow artists like Meaghan Blanchard, Tim Chaisson, and Dennis Ellsworth.

"We never get to see each other, except on the road, and we all live in this really small place, so I thought we should spend time with each other more. So, it's like community-building."

There is a co-writing temptation in the air which Catherine heretofore has rested aside—the box she has in her possession full of Gene's personal notes, thoughts, dreams, and numerous half-completed compositions, in lyrical form only, excerpts of which have been unearthed for the first time for this book. Although she hasn't tackled completing any of those unfinished Gene compositions, Catherine explains how when she is writing, she feels she is essentially always "co-writing" with her dad, and that there is always the possibility that she may someday purposefully open up that box and begin co-writing with him posthumously.

A previous biographical subject of mine, the late Newfoundland singer--songwriter Ron Hynes (in the 2016 book *One Man Grand Band*), always thought he would someday co-write with Gene. He was crushed when Gene died, realizing that it would never come to pass. Instead, to compensate to himself and provide a gift to Gene's followers, Hynes wrote and recorded the beautiful dedication to Gene, "Godspeed." It is one of Hynes's most loved songs and one of the ones he performed, with Catherine looking on, at that previously mentioned 2012 Zion Presbyterian Church CBC Radio and TV taping in Charlottetown. He was the only non-Islander who performed that night. A hidden anecdote about Hynes's appearance involved the fact that the people involved with the church were not happy with his performance of "Godspeed" because he sang the word "God damn" several more times than he was supposed to. Due to technical difficulties, he was forced to do three takes of the song, reciting "God damn. God damn," as part of the lyric goes, right there in the church.

Godspeed, Godspeed
Forgive a sweet soul a desperate deed
His was a prison and he was freed
Godspeed, Godspeed
God bless, God bless
What's born out of sorrow or out of distress
Speculation is anyone's guess
God bless, God bless
God only knows what takes a petal from the rose
What makes the dark rivers overflow
What makes a lifetime come and go
But God damn, God damn
You put your hand in the hand of the man
Must have believed he would understand
Forgive a sweet soul a desperate deed
Godspeed, Godspeed
God only knows what takes a petal from the rose
What makes the dark rivers over flow
What makes a lifetime come and go
But God damn, God damn
You put your hand in the hand of the man
Must have believed he would understand
Forgive a sweet soul a desperate deed
Godspeed, Godspeed
Godspeed

—By Ron Hynes, written in memory of Gene MacLellan

I found clarity and strength in the pages I would write
And I found I had my own thoughts, that yours weren't always mine
So I went back to the shadows of a winter in my home
And you watched my every move from behind the grave stone

—"Beneath the Lindens" by Catherine MacLellan

Who made the mountains Daddy
Who made the rivers and the sea
Who made the oceans Daddy
And poured them out for you and me
Who makes the poet and the king
And starts the birds to sing so early
   in the morning
Who makes the gold and silver
And hides it in the ground
Who made Niagara Daddy
With all that water comin' down

—Untitled, unpublished lyrics from Gene MacLellan's personal journals

CHAPTER 12

Together

N ot every father and daughter get to share a story. Or a stage.

"Ours is pretty entwined," says Catherine, "and especially lately, it seems like my whole life is about my dad. The year of Gene," she said, reflecting on this book, a documentary about her and her dad, her tribute album and her show of the same name, *If It's Alright With You.*

It's not that there's too much Gene, although for a long time Catherine was trying to, only figuratively, "get away from him," because she did not want to start her music career under the shadow of his fame. But that episode is long over.

"I think I got to a point where I was so comfortable with it and proud of what he did. You know, and that is around the time that I started playing 'Snowbird.' It's just very interesting, and I want to keep his music alive and his story alive because it keeps him alive in a way."

Gene is already kept alive in Catherine's face and demeanour.

Catherine likes to think she was the namesake of Gene's mother, even though her mother, Judith, says otherwise. There is an image of Catherine—

or Kay—in Catherine's Dixon Road home that is simply stunning. Catherine's features are from Gene's side of the family rather than her mom's.

"You know, part of what I take from what he did and from what I do is that if you follow your heart and your creative drive that you can make a life from it. I also happen to be focusing a lot on his and my mental-health stuff and that, although, it didn't end that well for him, it is within people's means to take care of themselves."

According to Judith, for the longest time, when Catherine first started out, she didn't want to have the connection between her and her dad to be known.

"She said, 'If I am going to do this, I am going to do this on my own. I am not going to go on the coattails on my father's fame.'"

But Catherine figured it all out.

"I think she knew all along it was a gift," says Judith, "but she just didn't want her career handed to her on a silver platter. And it would have been. And I think for five years, unless they really knew Catherine, most people didn't know that she had a famous father. And now she celebrates it because every time I turn around, she is singing one of his songs."

There was no real in-depth discussion around it.

"You just saw it happen. She's very much like her father was. Very quiet. She has his looks. She has his stage presence."

Of course the one thing Catherine will never do is perform with Gene, unless it's achieved artificially the way Natalie Cole did with her father, Nat King Cole, with the famous overlaid duet recording of "Unforgettable."

But that doesn't mean she can't be creative *with* him or be with him in her own way.

Every once in a while, Catherine makes a point of checking in spiritually with her dad, like when things are really tough with money or life's issues are weighing heavily on her. She has found a way to "talk" to him, asking, "Could you help me out? Please?"

In that vein, Catherine sees her dad as sort of a "ghostly sounding board."

"He's still around for sure. He's around in everything that I do in my writing, and there is a piece of him that like a thread that holds our family together."

Catherine's mother is also a sounding board, but mostly for observations and remembrances, as well as affirmations about what linkages existed or exist between Catherine and Gene, who spent a lot of time together, more so than the other two children.

"Philip was kind of off doing his thing," Judith says. "You know what teenage boys are like. They don't want to be around the house. They don't want to be near their dad. And Rachel was with a boy."

Driving back and forth for orthodontist appointments and the like, Gene and Catherine would talk. It was their thing and their space.

"I would never know what they were talking about," says Judith.

Then there was that time he took Catherine to Anne Murray's cottage in Nova Scotia.

"Anne was having a get-together with the *Singalong* crowd and he took Catherine with him," recalls Judith. "I don't think he was going to go. He decided at the last minute."

It was a rare event.

"I thought at the time I was kind of jealous; I was going, 'he must be mad at me. You didn't invite me to go.' But I was glad that he took somebody and I'm glad it was Catherine because I think it started a lot."

Judith says Gene's decision to take Catherine with him wasn't a plan. Even though the two were close, Catherine might simply have been the first person he saw in the house when he decided to go and ended up inviting her, she speculates.

"Who knows?" she says, indicating that with Gene there was no way to know what he was thinking most of the time.

Gene was neither close nor not close with Murray.

"I think it was the fact that it was the *Singalong* crew that was getting together that drove him over there. I wouldn't say that Anne and Gene were close at all."

Judith recalls hearing that Gene told Murray that he had a daughter who could sing.

"He just knew it...."

Catherine remembers the get-together with fondness. The *Singalong* crowd had lots of kids with them, most of whom were off playing. But Catherine clung close to her father as he and the other adults watched videos of themselves performing on TV and as they sang songs and traded stories.

"Basically I saw them as a real family," she recalls. "Dad had a good time."

Judith is fascinated with how the link continues, even now, between Catherine and her father.

"I often wonder how much of a stronger connection there would have been if Gene had lived until she was through high school," Judith says, "like in her early twenties starting out, what he would have told her, what she would have learned."

Judith says that in a way, Gene's journals are his way of speaking to her in lieu of his being there physically.

"She's had Gene's books for years in her basement, and she is just now reading them," all the annals of Gene's smallest and largest thoughts, sometimes expressing himself through Willard's voice, through partially finished lyrics, scores of random observations, and innocuous errand lists.

"It would have been interesting to see what Willard would have said," [to Catherine], Judith muses.

✳   ✳   ✳

Apart from personal memories, Catherine has evolved to think about togetherness with her father as involving his songs, which she describes as being "alive and well." Her decision to share herself through her music took courage and, frankly, guts.

"She believes in music," says Eric MacEwen. "She believes in love. I believe Catherine has a tremendous spiritual connection to her father on a daily basis; it grounds her, helps her carry on."

You brought the light into the dark and the sound of laughter
The joy back to my heart, what I was after
And though you may not know just what you did
You sheltered me from all that northeast wind

— "RUSHING WINDING WIND" BY CATHERINE MACLELLAN

18
5
9 0

JUST A LITTLE TALK WITH JESUS
JUST A CLOSER WALK WITH THEE
HAND IN THE HAND
THE REUNION SONG
ELIJAH
LOOKIN' FOR A MIRACLE
HIGHER GROUND   (Pg. 1) #3
I DON'T MIND   (Pg. 53) #3
AMAZING GRACE
PEACE IN THE VALLEY   (107) #3
SWEET BY AND BY   (155) #3
SOFTLY AND TENDERLY   (209) #3
WHITER THAN SNOW (213) #3
WHISPER A PRAYER (241) #3
WHAT A FRIEND   (272) #3
BATTLE HYMN OF THE REPUBLIC (298) #3

It's a cold day but it's sunny

The wind is high and the trees are still

It's a cold day but it's sunny

The wind is high and the trees are still

You don't need imagination

To believe me when I say I've had my fill

—Untitled, unpublished lyrics from Gene MacLellan's personal journals

CHAPTER 13

THE EVOLUTION
OF CATHERINE

Given his withdrawn nature, it's hard to explain how it is that Gene could project charisma and personal magnetism. It was just there. He didn't do a lot of banter. He just sang his songs, but there was something about him that drew people in.

It's said that you either have it or you don't have it. They say Johnny Cash had it off the scale. And Dean Martin. And others at the top of their performance or political craft, like former US president Bill Clinton, who was blessed. But with most magnetic people, charisma presents itself in a dynamic outward action.

In Gene's case, it's even more of a mysterious, ineffable quality than what we normally experience. Psychiatrists explain charisma as the quality of people who connect to others through confidence, exuberance, optimism, expressive body language, and a friendly, passionate voice. The latter might have applied to Gene.

The notion that Catherine has any hint of charisma is abstract to her.

"That to me is amazing," she says, admitting that she has no idea what her best performance qualities are. That's for others to decide, she believes.

"Lennie Gallant did once tell me the first time he saw me play, he saw that same thing my dad had, that kind of quiet thing that engaged people. I don't know what it is, but he said I had that. And that's what I hear.

"Sometimes I play at Baba's [Lounge] in Charlottetown, where it seems that you could never shut down the crowd to be quiet and listen, but they would stop talking. The whole room would stop."

She didn't know what it was she was doing that would cast a spell over the room, but it would happen again and again.

"It's rare that I have to play through a talking audience, but I also tend to play places that have that built in," places like Baba's aside.

She observes that one aspect of her comfort at Baba's and her ability to hold people's attention is that they were her people. They were *her* crowd. That is where local musician, entrepreneur, and talent producer Pat Deighan got to know Catherine. He recalls that she was playing Baba's with the New Drifts, the group she formed with James Phillips, Stéphane Bouchard, and Dave Gould.

Deighan had first met Catherine in his early twenties at a Gene MacLellan tribute that Scott Parsons put on at Victoria-by-the-Sea. Deighan was playing in a band at the time called Strawberry, a little indie rock outfit that was working the East Coast.

"It was pretty wild, I mean, the first time we laid eyes on Catherine and we heard her onstage, there was something very special about her. I am thinking early 2000s, 2003, 2004, maybe a little earlier. Seeing Catherine and hearing her voice, it was just immediate. It was immediate she had talent. She had it. She was great onstage at a young age too."

Springboarding from that Victoria-by-the-Sea concert, Deighan has had the good fortune of watching Catherine develop as an artist from the time of her initial appearances at Baba's lounge to her first CD, through to today.

"Catherine and I have always had a great relationship. I think it was early on that I kind of knew my talent level and how far I could take it, like friends and other people in the music scene. But I think sometimes someone comes along, like a Catherine, and it's cliché to say it, where you're like, 'Wow, she's really good'—a beautiful voice and a great stage presence."

Baba's Lounge was the centre of their musical worlds back in the day, all part of the same scene. Everybody in the Island music scene cut their teeth there.

"Baba's has been Catherine's place, like other Island artists," says Deighan. "I think I performed there when I was seventeen with a guy playing bass. That was our bar for a long time. I always played there and we would always go there to see similar people who'd blow our minds, Mitch Schurman being one and Chas Gay."

Those guys taught Deighan and others in his peer group a lot about music. In those early Baba's days, Deighan would be up front singing songs, but he tired of it.

"I just got sick and tired of fronting a band and I wanted to disappear, and drums were a passion. I've been doing drums now for like twelve to fourteen years."

Today, Deighan continues to drum in a party band called The Love Junkies. But back to those references of entrepreneur and talent producer, he spends most of his time running Back Alley Music in downtown Charlottetown—PEI's go-to-trendy vinyl music store— and the Trailside Music Café and Inn in rural Mount Stewart, the website for which reads "it's just you, the musicians and the warmth of good food and drink," which is a perfectly honest descriptor for the Trailside. Catherine has played there ever since Deighan and his wife, Megan, took it over several years ago. She does three or more good solid shows there every summer, says Deighan, all of which sell out immediately.

"Megan and I always describe Catherine as one of the perfect Trailside shows in the sense that she puts on a very nice and relaxing performance. 'Spellbinding' is a good word that comes up a lot. She just captures the Trailside's mood, which is laid-back and relaxed, like a nice warm blanket that falls over you. There is something about Catherine and the Trailside that fit well together. There's been a lot of special shows with Catherine there."

✷   ✷   ✷

Deighan's performance background, his producer background at the Trailside and other shows he stages, and his involvement with Back Alley Music, gives him a perspective like no one else on understanding the appeal about Gene's and Catherine's music.

"There are a lot of people looking for Gene's music," says Deighan. "When the vinyl comes in, it is sold fast. It's always the first and second albums. There is one compilation, *Lonesome River*, I do believe it's called, and that's the one CD we haven't been able to get in for years. Availability has dried up. We couldn't keep them in stock. After that, the vinyl comes in used when I buy peoples' collections. Anytime it comes in though, especially the first album, which is magnificent, it just sells fast. People are looking for it—people who know music and who know songwriters. It is a brilliant album. It's insane."

Deighan has of course also sold Catherine's music at Back Alley from day one.

"It's been amazing to watch Catherine. I mean, we all look forward to Catherine's CDs. We knew the songs, we'd see her play all the time. It was pretty exciting, and now, it's just interesting to watch an artist grow from CD to CD to CD; it's a nice thing to witness.

"I mean, like any artist, you gain your confidence over the years with recording, with writing, with performing. I've seen her grow into that art-ist. But I mean—she was always captivating onstage. We'd always love to see Catherine. Her voice was just always a beautiful voice. I mean—it was great. She's always someone I followed as a songwriter. I write myself, so I'd always listen to her album. I was excited to hear what she was writing and writing about different directions.

"I think Catherine is continuing to grow as an artist. I think she is striving to write amazing songs. I think in this day and age, who knows what you can do to make it in the music industry, but I think she is in it for the long haul to be a great artist and to write good songs."

✼   ✼   ✼

Catherine says that controlling or engaging a crowd is a learned thing.

"You engage a crowd by relating to them and with them, and trying to work at having a set list that isn't all one note and having banter that kind of makes people laugh between sad songs."

She admits that if you have something that really works, you tend to go back to that again and again.

"I never use the exact same thing, but I'll try to get the same kind of message across. If I am telling the story of a song, then I'll use it for a while, and then it will trickle into something else."

While songwriting is her first true love, it is surprising, given her quiet nature, that she enjoys performing.

"I love performing, which is weird because I was such a shy kid. I used to get nervous. Really bad nerves, but then I just barrelled through it. Kind of the same way when I went to Australia and I didn't cry or anything. Now I get excited. Instead of a numbness though, it's a grounded-ness. It's like an excited grounded-ness."

Oddly, Catherine loves being in photographs, either posing with fans or doing publicity shoots, which is contradictory to her extreme shyness as a young girl and her earlier performance apprehensions.

Early on, Catherine's stage talk was originally limited to, "this song is called" and the proverbial "and it goes a little something like this"—and little else.

"It wasn't very engaging. But I guess I am just maturing. I am older now. I know more of who I am. I really love people and I love finding that common ground with people.

"Although my stage banter is getting better, so you make them laugh in between songs."

Catherine credits Lennie Gallant as being helpful with her stagecraft.

"And Ron [Hynes] was a big one who taught me about how to hold the stage. Because nobody could hold the stage like Ron could. He could just stand on the stage and not say anything and people would listen and wait."

Hynes died in November of 2015 of an uncalculated combination of cancer and drug abuse.

Catherine jokes that a lot of people would remain silent because they were terrified to talk or joke around when Hynes was onstage. That's only partly a joke. Hynes was known to seriously lash out verbally at people who made noise during his shows.

"There was part of that, right? I mean he intimidated the audience, but he was a master storyteller, and could engage a crowd like nobody else I've ever seen. I was in awe of him anytime we got a chance to tour together. He was amazing.

"I guess the most common feedback I get is that people like my shows because they seem to get a sense of peace or they can relate to what I do. I think that is the biggest thing for me is when someone comes up and says that a song made them cry. Then I know that I've reached them in that, although I didn't know when I was starting out that my goal would be to reach other people. That is so validating; it's like my personal experience, or my personal view on the world, could reach somebody who has a different life experience that we can share that connection."

Her songs are generally pretty serious, employing important and emotional subject matter. As odd as it sounds, she loves having the ability to make people cry in public.

✳   ✳   ✳

Catherine can't explain how she found the connective place with her audience.

"I just kept doing it until I got so used to doing it that it was okay, and I knew I wasn't going to die. I'm not shy on the stage anymore. I was for a long time. Like I couldn't even look at the audience. I would just like, shoegaze. I was a classic shoegazer and I would never say a word."

Gene was no shoegazer, Catherine says. He was no comedian, but he looked out on the crowd. Not necessarily at them, but on them.

Judith MacLellan cannot get over her daughter's ability to be onstage performing before several hundred people. She loves being there for the thrill.

"The difference between Gene and Catherine is that Gene loved the music, but he didn't like necessarily being onstage with it. When she first started out, you could tell how nervous and quiet she was, but now that she has found herself stage-wise, she's broken through that. She's evolving every year. That's what amazes me. She evolves every year. Every time I see her onstage, I just go, 'Oh my gosh, that's my daughter.' I don't know how she does it. I could never do it."

Which is how most average people would feel about being onstage as exposed as Catherine has made herself.

Catherine didn't really see her dad perform very often.

"He would usually play things like school variety shows for us because he was kind and generous and did benefits on the Island, and then I saw him once play at the rink in North Rustico with Lennie Gallant. And I saw him play at a festival in Ontario somewhere. He took me up to Ontario. Looking back, it was like, he just sat there with the guitar and he sang, and there was no *show* about it. But it was engaging nonetheless."

Any remaining traces of shoegazing were dashed by Catherine in the summer of 2017 when she began her summer-long run of her tribute to Gene, mirroring the album released on June 30 of that year: *If It's Alright With You.*

The PEI Brewing Company performance space in Charlottetown had the capacity to seat 240 people per night over more than thirty shows, most of which were sold out. The production marked a large moment in the arc of Catherine's career. She vaulted her stage presence and her voice to new levels and opened her heart to her audiences, reflecting honestly about life with her father, the foibles and great things about him, personal memories, and speaking frankly about mental health. Audiences held their arms open to her.

Collaborator John Connolly says that when he and Catherine began working on the script for the production, they agreed that if she was going to tell her father's story, she needed "to be honest in all respects."

And she was and she is.

"As difficult as it was for her to sift through some of the challenging details of the past," Connolly wrote in the show's house programme, "Catherine showed tremendous courage and resolve in her desire to shine a light into her father's story and open up a broader conversation about mental health."

The show includes video clips of Gene talking and a couple of the very few photographs which exist of him with the family, in spite of the fact that one of his "bursts of creativity," as Catherine put it, involved his love of photography as one of his non-musical creative outlets, as was the case with drawing. Gene was always the one photographing the other members of the family, which is why there are hardly any images of him with wife Judith and the kids: he was always the one behind the lens. Gene had a 35 mm Pentax with a zoom lens which Catherine still has in her possession.

"My dad was really into it, and I guess I was aware of it as a thing. I mean we all had little disposable cameras. I always loved having one."

The whole photography thing had an effect on her, even though his photographs weren't very good.

"Before I moved to Toronto, I tried to figure out what I wanted to do with my life because I had quit university and thought I could take a photography course. I got my application all ready, and I did up my little portfolio of pictures, and that was super fun. But I ended up not even applying to the course. I always fooled around with it. I had a darkroom at one point with equipment borrowed from a friend."

For Catherine's mother, it was astonishing to see her daughter performing Gene's music and speaking so openly about their lives. To a degree, she left speechless.

"What can I say about this show?" Judith asks. "It is one of the best I have seen in the past few years, although I am just a bit biased," she jokes. "It brings back great memories.

"She amazes me. She absolutely amazes me. That whole Gene thing. I have a picture of her and it's like somebody Photoshopped her dad, and they are both in this picture, and they are both looking the same way, and you can tell they have the same profile. She has a lot of her father in her. Quiet. Deep thinker.

Carnival Queen

Sharon Ritcey is crowned Queen of The 1972 Lunenburg High School Winter Carnival by song writer Gene MacLellan. The Crowning was the final ceremony of the three day Carnival which ended on Saturday. Mr. MacLellan's appearance in Lunenburg was sponsored by the Student Council. Photo by Terry G. Conrad.

There are not many candid photos of Gene, but his family has newspaper clippings such as this one from 1972 in Lunenburg, Nova Scotia, where Gene had been invited to crown the Carnival Queen.

Gene was a deep thinker. All my kids amaze me, but Catherine amazes me the most. The fact that she is doing what she is doing and sticking with it. I mean, she doesn't make a heck of a lot of money, but she makes ends meet."

Of course, Judith went to see the production more than once.

"The last time I went I realized that this would be the first time the grandchildren would have heard Gene's voice," thanks to segments of the production which feature audio of Gene speaking.

"They have heard him sing but never in conversation. They all leave feeling they have come a little bit closer to knowing who their grandfather was. 'Amazing' is the common word used by all of them."

By the end of the show's run, seven of the eight grandchildren would have seen the show. The youngest, only five years of age, may get a chance yet now that there will be a second year's run.

"This show should be seen by everyone who loves music and or remembers Gene," says Judith. "There is laughter, sadness, and a whole lot of emotions in between! The musicians, sound, and light people are the best anywhere. Their contributions are making this show a success! I am so very proud of Catherine."

Instead of experiencing sadness or trepidation, Judith has been lifted by Catherine's show. And she had no idea regarding the approach or the content, right up to opening night, on July 3, 2017.

"Catherine did a great job of keeping her songs and plans for the show from me until the last few weeks before it opened. I am always amazed at how well Catherine vocalizes what is most dear to her heart. I have felt many emotions—sadness that Gene is gone and that he did not receive the help he needed, but happy that we get a glimpse of the man. It brings back the feeling that maybe I could have helped him more but, at the same time, knowing that I couldn't. I find myself chuckling and outright laughing at some of the pictures and stories. My memories come rolling back big time."

Marty Reno made a point of getting to Catherine's tribute. It was an overwhelming experience for him.

"The way Catherine presented him at her concert, I tell you, my heart was just pumping," says Reno. "It was just like he was there with me and it was so wonderful...the way she told the story, and everybody that was there really got to know him a lot better than they ever thought they would. Nobody knew him in such a great light as she showed during that concert."

Reno says watching Catherine was hard. It brought tears to his eyes throughout the performance.

"Not in sadness," he says, "but in joy that she was telling that just like it is, you know. And when she sang and played, and the whole thing was, to me, the most wonderful concert I've even been to because of there was something in everything about the presentation. And Catherine had such sincerity that it just brought him back to life. It was wonderful for me in a lot of ways that I just can't get over."

Reno says Catherine's interpretation of Gene's songs shows that she understands where those songs come from.

"Like if you really want to know Gene," he says, "if you just listen to all those songs, they were the life he lived. She knows that. I know she must have been very close to him in his last years because she spent a lot of time with him when she was older so she probably had a lot of private conversations with him that must have been wonderful. She reminds me so much of him it's uncanny."

Reno is referring not only to their physical resemblance but their personas too, the gentleness and the humility.

"I surely see Gene in Catherine," says Reno. "It's just like being with Gene when I'm with her."

Reno says Gene viewed his success humbly, believing he had just lucked out.

"It took years for him to realize his talent was a God-given thing that he had to share. She's gotten to that point already and she's young compared to where Gene was when he realized that's what he was meant to be doing. She's just very much like him, and you can see in the ways that she treats her daughter. She's a beautiful soul."

Catherine knew Reno was in the audience that night, which he agrees probably made that particular show doubly difficult and doubly emotional for her.

"It probably was," says Reno, "but she's so gentle, she's such a dear person, and she just made me feel right at home as if I was part of the family again.

I'd been gone for a long time, so it was like being home and like watching your little girl who's all grown up doing this stuff, these amazing things."

Reno got to the show, spent time at Catherine's Dixon Road home and her studio, and was able to mingle with the band.

He says he couldn't imagine how Catherine could do so many successive shows about such a powerfully emotional aspect of life. He remarked about how during the show, when she laughed at something funny Gene had said, it sounded like she was laughing at it for the first time.

✳   ✳   ✳

Launching *If It's Alright With You* was a special moment in time for Catherine's music career.

"I didn't know what to expect when we started working on the show in December [2016]. By the time we were in rehearsals, I was not ready at all, and then the first night we hit the stage, and I was like, 'Oh, we can do this.' You know, it was still rough, like the first couple of weeks. I felt like I was still learning the show. We only had two weeks of rehearsals before the show started."

Rehearsals took place mostly at the Dixon Road recording studio, followed by just a few twelve-hour days at the Brewing Company venue. She learned from the experience that it was not nearly enough rehearsal time and probably would prefer not to repeat that mistake.

"For the first few weeks of the show, I did not feel I was owning it at all. I was just like I tried to remember my lines and remember the songs and the chords, and it felt a lot of moving pieces all coming together."

Audiences, however, did not seem to pick up on any apprehensions Catherine felt.

Reflective of the scale of what the show has achieved is that people came from all over to see her and hear about Gene's music and life. Many made the show into their singular reason for visiting PEI in 2017.

"It is just the scale of that, you know, to see people coming in from wher-ever. It's definitely the biggest thing I've ever done. It is totally different."

Audiences were getting two shows in one—one Catherine's and one Gene's.

"Now I am owning it and it feels so exciting. There are a couple of moments I just love, like the end of the first half when I walk off the stage, it is like a super rock-and-roll moment because the band is still playing."

In spite of the joy the tribute has given Catherine, the show has also been hard.

"It has the same kind of feeling every night where the first half is so happy and easy and it is like things are great. Life is good."

This is before the show moves into the matter of her father's mental health and his suicide.

"The second half, you can tell there is a bit of tension and then I go off stage, John [Connolly] sings 'Puerto Vallarta' and when I come back on, I love that sensation. The last two speeches are really hard, so I kind of have this *I can't even think about it* even before I do it.

"I knew I had to talk about the end of Dad's life and mental health is a huge thing to me, and it's something that I talk about. I've done actual talks on mental health, but I don't want to be heavy handed" while she still wants to be entertaining people.

"I don't know about how surprised people are. They definitely don't see it coming. In the first half, there is just nothing but cherries and roses. You know. And then the second half, things start going there. I mean it just naturally does because of the arc of his life, you know. Anyway. It wasn't something I set out to do. It almost seemed like it was out of my control. It was like...I can't tell his story without telling that and speaking up."

Thirty-eight at the time of this writing, Catherine is a clear-headed champion for the cause of mental health. Not just because of her father's experience, but also because of her own experience, captured as she was, but freed from the unpredictable grip of depression. One can believe that with each new MacLellan generation, the individuals get stronger, Gene transitioning to Catherine and now strong, independent Isabel.

As evoked in Gene's "Shilo Song," Catherine is old enough to know that when her dad is *around*, you can feel their love still grow, that she can be herself and let it go. His legacy to her has made her happy. And for anyone

A young Gene with a guitar embarking on the career that made him famous.
(Courtesy of Bud King)

having the chance to see her perform and smile, together Gene and Catherine possess a magic that makes it worthwhile.

"Dad has been the biggest gift for me," says Catherine, who welcomed the opportunity to talk openly and on such a personal level.

"The biggest thing I get feedback wise is just so many people saying, 'Thank you for sharing that story. Thank you for talking about that because I'm bipolar,' or 'My daughter took her life.'"

There is no end to the stories which stream from her fans following each performance. Recognizing the importance of this connection, Catherine meets people at the back of the performance venue each and every night.

"I realized a few weeks into the show that this show requires a lot more of me than any other show I've done," referring to both the physical and emotional demands of the performance and the emotional draw of spending close-up time with so many fans. Catherine spent the summer of 2017 suspended in some space between her strength and her vulnerability. It's one thing to stand strong and singularly hold centrestage before 240 people, but as she put it, "I also have to be in this vulnerable place to tell the story. Otherwise, it doesn't come across with honesty."

She reflects on her ability to "come into work" and experience such a beautiful thing among herself, her dad, and their fans. It is a metaphor for how Catherine seeks to live her life day to day.

✖   ✖   ✖

As author and required observer of Catherine, it is clear to me that the tribute show has sent Catherine to another strata. The spellbinding performer from good old reliable Baba's Lounge was still intact as she began the evening with her haunting solo rendition of "Snowbird," the same sense of softness and quiet you get by watching most of her YouTube videos. But she magnifies herself manifold with each number that follows. If she is five-foot-something at the opening number, she is one hundred feet tall by the time she's done. If her musical stature whispers at the strike of the first piano note in that opening of "Snowbird," she is symphonic in stature by the close of the second act and that last syllable of "Put Your Hand in the Hand."

I spoke to Catherine after one of her shows, asking if she understood just how much bigger she is onstage in *If It's Alright With You* compared with other performances I'd seen. After a light joking reference to food and diet, it seemed to me she may not truly comprehend the degree to which this is so.

Perhaps the evolution of Catherine in 2017 cannot be measured.

But now what? What about after the end of this show, which she admits cannot go on forever any more than she would wish for it to? Catherine has old but new career questions to face: If the Gene material is removed from her next phase as a singer-songwriter and musician, how *big* will she seem without it? After being cast on the "big screen" that this show has afforded her, how will she employ her traditional musical stock-in-trade moving forward? What will she write and perform that will continue to build a legacy? Can she do so by retreating to the basic qualities, which so many people say made her father's music and persona so special and hers likewise?

It's like, after sold-out houses at Carnegie Hall, what does it feel like to be back in a small Greenwich Village bar? Understanding the arc of a music career and having to have the next big thing occur, what is Catherine's next thing? Balance that against her refusal to be anything but true to herself and her own music, continuing to build success will assuredly be a challenge.

Before the show had wrapped in September of 2017, Catherine was busy booking a mini Ontario tour of the tribute, which saw performances in the Peterborough area and in Ottawa at the National Arts Centre. She did so without benefit of management or agents and anticipates more touring, in Atlantic Canada or elsewhere, following her second brewing company run in 2018 in Charlottetown.

"I don't know. I waver. I think I like the self-management for the most part, and right now, this show has kind of taken over my life so I haven't had much managing to do."

✳   ✳   ✳

Anticipating the closure of the first run of the show in September 2017, and wondering how she would resume the rest of her career, two things started to sink in—that she would have a lot of her own new writing to do and that the entire experience altered her perspective on how she can play piano and guitar and sing.

"Career-wise, for me right now, is focusing on how to grow the tribute show for the short term because I don't see this is something I can do for a long time. I will probably get a few years out of it, which is great. I have an album that's waiting to be made of my own material, so trying to find the time to do that is challenging. We will do it at home in our studio."

Six weeks before the run wound up, she was "super excited" about getting back to writing.

"Normally, I write throughout the year," she reflects, "but this had been the longest period without writing because I have been so busy writing and working on the show.

"It's been good to take a break from my own stuff. I think that's the biggest thing for me. I wasn't sure how I would feel about that, but it's a really nice break. It's like going on vacation from yourself.

"When I write, I'm typically writing at home in my comfort zone and vocally in my comfort zone too. My dad's songs are totally different from that. Like, he sang differently. He had different vocal tricks and it is so fun to sing his songs."

Close friend Tara MacLean has a keen eye on the arc of Catherine's career.

"You know, it is clear to me having knowing her work so well, she is going to become another Canadian legend. She is truly brilliant, and when I sit there and watch her play, I just want to weep because I am just so grateful that she exists that she has such a deep and powerful poet."

MacLean calls Canada a funny place to be a musician, especially for women. They spend years "pounding the pavement," playing countless gigs over many years, paying their dues, having to scratch and fight for government assistance. She compares Canada's system to the US star system, pointing out the gap between how artists are recognized.

"At the level we are at, we would be superstars in the States," she says.

But they keep on pushing and creating, like the way Catherine found a new frontier of creativity involving her dad and his music—now their music.

"I think that Catherine is being recognized and I think just as more time goes on," says MacLean, "and the more she plays, especially with this show is perfect because she gets to do something which was a dream of hers, to share the story of her dad."

At the same time, she gets to work for her cause, helping people understand and remove the stigma of mental illness. Gene's music and life story have served as a pathway to Catherine and her originality, to her music, her sound, and her increasingly larger presence.

"She is such a great musician," says MacLean. "She is so authentic and real and lovely. I think she is just going to get better and better. She just won a Juno last year, and you know, she and Chris are such an amazing pair working together. Yeah, I think this is just the beginning for Catherine. I love that I have an up-close seat to witness her success because it is just going to keep getting better. She is going to pick up where her dad left off. You know in the sense that he wasn't able to get well. He wasn't able to be well and she is, you know. She is. She is strong and smart, powerful and she is going to make music forever."

> No one ever said it would be easy
> Nothing in this life comes for free
> I will do my best to try and catch you
> When you're falling away from me
>
> —"HOLD ON" BY CATHERINE MACLELLAN

Scrabble

Score sheet

Rachel	Dad	Catherine

ACKNOWLEDGEMENTS

Every authorized biography calls upon the trust and patience of the subject. There are not enough words to describe the degree to which Catherine MacLellan has been trusting of my work and patient with my countless inquiries and visits to her home in Breadalbane. She is one of the warmest and most beautiful people I have ever met. Special thanks also to Judith MacLellan for opening up her heart to this story. To everyone who collaborated with me in telling this story about Catherine and her dad, Gene, there are not enough ways to express my thanks. Thanks also to Nimbus publisher Terrilee Bulger and editor Elaine McCluskey for recognizing the value and beauty of this story and for their patience and guidance throughout the writing process. Finally, thank you to my partner, Charlotte Stewart, who for more than a decade has endured the now-predictable trials of watching me write, always providing sound and insightful criticism because she is the reader in the midst.

ABOUT THE AUTHOR

Harvey Sawler was born and grew up in Hamilton, Ontario, but has lived most of his life in Atlantic Canada. He began writing as an eighteen-year-old newspaper reporter covering stories as diverse as the funerals of two murdered Moncton city police officers, interviewing disgraced Canadian hockey agent and promoter Alan Eagleson, and working aboard the 1974 Pierre Trudeau whistle-stop campaign train, with infant son Justin in his arms and wife, Margaret, at his side, as they crossed northern New Brunswick. He has written more than a dozen books, including three novels and non-fiction projects such as *Twenty-First Century Irvings*, *Frank McKenna: Beyond Politics*, *Last Canadian Beer: The Moosehead Story*, and *One Man Grand Band-The Lyrical Life of Ron Hynes*. His biographical account of Canadian blues legend Dutch Mason (*On The Road With Dutch Mason* with co-author David Bedford) will be premiered as an original Canadian musical at the 2018 Charlottetown Festival. He is currently completing *Pluck and Luck*, the biography focusing on the life of Canadian promoter, theatre impresario, and thoroughbred horse-racing fanatic John Uren. He is also a leading Canadian tourism and marketing consultant. Harvey lives at Bellevue Cove, Prince Edward Island, with his partner, Charlotte Stewart. You can visit him any time at www.harveysawler.com.